The Road to Revision

How the

~~Proposed Revision of the~~

Form of Government

Came To Be

Foreword

I was born and raised in the small village of Cambria, Wisconsin, where the Presbyterian Church reflected strongly the Welsh-American tradition of Wesleyan piety and Calvinistic polity of 19th century Wales. I received a degree in history from Macalester College in St. Paul, Minnesota. Pittsburgh Theological Seminary granted a Bachelor of Divinity degree in 1970 and McCormick Theological Seminary allowed a Doctor of Ministry degree in 1988.

I was ordained to the "Gospel Ministry" in 1970 and I served as a parish pastor through 1986 and again from 1992 until retirement in 2008. The middle period included terms as a presbytery Stated Clerk and as an interim Executive Presbyter in the presbyteries of Winnebago, Long Island and Lackawanna. As a retired person, my wife Carole and I live in the home in which I grew up. A large garden provides vegetables for table and freezer. A community band has gotten the clarinet once again out of its case. An occasional (often enough but not too often) supply preaching opportunity keeps the rust from growing on the vocal chords and the mind.

To all who have nurtured and challenged my crazy love for polity, to my spouse, children and cherished friends I am extremely grateful. If a few folk out there find this review of 20 years of polity discussion helpful in shaping their own opinions, I will be pleased.

Cambria, Wisconsin
December 2011

Table of Contents

Introduction: A Place Where I Begin

In retirement I live in the home where I grew up in south central Wisconsin. My wife and I have ten acres of ground and I have a large garden. Frankly, while gardening is work, the feel of cool soil between my fingers and the taste of food we've grown ourselves is a wondrous joy after 40 years of service in the church. We worship in a dynamic congregation at the center of the village. Getting the good news proclaimed and enacted takes precedence over polity, as well it should.

But I also live in the ecclesiastical "home" in which I grew up, the Presbyterian Church (U.S.A.). In 1981, having completed a three year "cycle" of Vice Moderator, Moderator, Immediate Past Moderator of my presbytery, I was asked to chair a committee to revise the presbytery's by-laws. In light of the approach of the long-hoped-for Reunion of the denomination I determined to undertake a serious study of the polity being proposed for the church. At the very least I was curious about this document although I took it at face value. In a year or so the by-laws were written and approved and life went on and reunion happened. In 1984 I was elected to be the Stated Clerk of Twin Cities Area Presbytery and my education in polity moved up a notch.

At meetings of clerks from around the church, confusion and frustration was often the order of the day. Changes had come. At first blush people assumed that practices unfamiliar had been simply the practice of the "other side". Sometimes that was the case. Then again things came up which no one saw as having been part of "our tradition." The evolution of the reunion documents (documents that had some of their genesis in the proposed reunion of three strands of historic Presbyterianism scheduled for 1958) is yet to be thoroughly documented in writing. But it came to be clear that more than a simple fusion of two existing documents was involved. In response, people sought the security of "the way we used to do it!" By 1989 the chorus of voices calling for a comprehensive review grew loud enough to generate action. A study committee was formed and went to work. It is the evolution of that effort that I am attempting to document here.

Let me be clear with the reader; what follows is not an "academic" historical study, nor is it a theological treatise on Presbyterian polity. As I have been directly involved in the movement to complete a comprehensive revision of the Form of Government, this is a personal reflection. I observed the early stages as an administrative staff person in presbyteries and as an interested "polity wonk" pastor. Since 1996 I was involved "hands on" in the creation of the proposed revision that was adopted in 2011. What I have attempted is a documentary memoir of the issues underlying revision and the way I have perceived them. I hope this reflective review will shed light on both the process by which the work proceeded as well as the polity that underlies our practice. I am thankful for God's invitation to be a part of it.

Part I: The Nature of the Church and the Practice of Governance

Chapter One: In the Beginning [1]

On January 7, 2010, on NPR's "Morning Edition" I heard a report of California Governor Arnold Schwarzenegger's State of the State message which I assume was delivered the day before. As I listened, the Governor said something to this effect: What does it say about our state that it spends more on prison uniforms than on caps and gowns....never again should we spend more on prisons than on higher education. He then proposed a Constitutional amendment that would mandate that state expenditures on higher education always exceed expenditures on prisons. [The Christian Science Monitor reported that California prisons at that time received 11% of the budget while higher education received 7%.]

Cool! Good idea! I would certainly be in favor, were I a Californian. But, as the news reporter noted: California already has the longest state constitution in America, a myriad of laws that some say explains why the budget is forever unbalanced. You see, they have, by legislation and referendum, created a CONSTITUTION that restricts flexible responses to contemporary problems. The legislature must do certain things, even if they cannot be afforded. The legislature is prohibited from doing certain things, even if they are wise and necessary. Only by Constitutional Amendment can things change. Gridlock and looming bankruptcy are the result.

OK, I don't know all the ins and outs of California politics. And I know they are more complicated than the simple-minded paragraph above. But......

The reason the PCUSA engaged in a 20 year push to differentiate within our Form of Government (FOG) the truly foundational principles from the Manual of Operations provisions is an effort to address a parallel problem. Sessions and presbyteries feel constrained by a "one size fits all" approach to solving problems. When confronted with something new, we have looked to the FOG for a prescriptive response, and if we did not find it we overtured [I shall assume that the vast majority of readers are Presbyterian and familiar with words we use; that is, to "overture" as a verb, is to request some action by a governing body] the General Assembly to amend the Constitution to solve our particular problem.

To illustrate the extent to which this can become trivial – a particular presbytery was confounded by a particular minister who aggravated the leadership of the presbytery greatly. After years of frustration, the minister in question asked to be "honorably retired", the phrase used in the Constitution at such times. The presbytery was not at all pleased to be constrained to call this person "honorable" anything. So, they sent an overture to the General Assembly that the Constitution be amended to strike the word "honorable" and make such an accolade an option but not required. Needless to say the vast majority of (presumably honorable) Honorably Retired ministers rose up in opposition. The matter was defeated. Such is the way it has been, and on many more substantive matters as well.

I would not wish to burden my analogy to California further. What I affirm is that our challenge is to recognize that problems are situationally unique and solutions need to be adaptive. Adaptive solutions need to rely on a shared set of Foundational Principles to which we refer not a set of cookie-cutter answers to complex questions.

How it all began [2]

Chuck Hammond was Moderator of the General Assembly of the United Presbyterian Church in the United States of America (UPCUSA) in one of the years immediately preceding reunion in 1983. I suppose one could say he was "plain spoken", "direct", "forthright", or some other such euphemism of kindness. The hard reality was that he was not a quiet person and could say the most outrageous things. They were accurate and true, and he was one who saw the big picture and could describe it well.

The 1989 Bicentennial Assembly was held in Philadelphia. I can still see Chuck as he went to the microphone reserved for former Moderators. I can still hear him as he spoke to the Assembly. He reviewed how our reunited church had been together only 5+ years and already the number of overtures to amend the Constitution grew exponentially, year by year, as people sought to put back into the book some rule or regulation they felt we could not live without. The matter of whether a candidate should be ordained in the "presbytery of care" or the "presbytery of call" had already switched back and forth a couple of times! Chuck's grasp of the breadth of these many changes and the effect such micro-managing had on our life together was comprehensive. His laundry list of issues was overwhelming and convincing. The Assembly acted to address the situation. It was a grand speech and the commissioners responded with action. But it was not his speech alone that moved the Assembly; the momentum to take action already had a broader context.

Three – seemingly – unrelated urges

Staging meetings of the General Assembly had evolved from a simple administrative duty fulfilled by the Office of the Stated Clerk to more complex mix of ecclesiastical and programmatic business. In the years around reunion the task fell to a small group of folk called the "Program Committee". The Stated Clerk, the Moderator of the (just past) Assembly, the Chair of the Local Arrangements Committee were the types of folks involved. In the days before Reunion, the PCUS, or "Southern Church", held its meetings on college campuses. The UPCUSA, or "Northern Church", had met in convention centers in major cities. Needless to say the costs and complexities varied greatly. Even in the north before reunion concern had been expressed to cut costs. The urge to reduce expenses also brought up the choice to hold meetings only every other year. The Program Committee had been directed to think on these matters and report to the 1989 Assembly.

That 1988 directive, known as "Referral C" was to study "The Nature and Purpose of the General Assembly". In September of that year, the committee met and determined to lump the referral with other concerns and launch a more expanded study. The Committee on the Office of the General Assembly (another name for essentially the same people as the Program Committee, hereafter referred to by its initials, COGA) asked the Theology and Worship Ministry Unit to collaborate on the study of the "Nature of the Church and the Practice of its Government", thus to provide a "sound theological framework." Because of the limited number of persons involved and as the scope of this proposed study was a bit outside the normal scope of work, COGA thought it wise to get a direct GA mandate. That request was what was brought in 1989 as a response to the referral.

At the same time, friction was developing within the newly consolidated "headquarters" building at 100 Witherspoon Street in Louisville. For the first few years of reunion the two former streams had sort-of carried on, gradually bringing leadership teams and elected folks together to shape and form this new denomination. One area of apparent friction revolved around the division between the ecclesiastical business of the church (represented by the Office of the General Assembly and the Stated Clerk) and the programmatic business of the church (represented by the General Assembly Council and the person of the Executive Director). The way the offices were historically construed, the Stated Clerk saw himself as a direct servant of the Assembly, accountable only to the Assembly and operating with funds directly levied by the Assembly from the presbyteries. (In those days the *per capita* assessment was very nominal amount and subject of not much objection.)

Now, for the first time since reunion, all entities, programmatic and ecclesiastical, shared the same physical space. "Modern" management tools were seeking efficiency of operation and consistency of policy. Suddenly, it appeared that the Stated Clerk needed to ask permission of others to carry out the essential functions of the office that were mandated to him by the Constitution and the General Assembly. This would not do. James Andrews, not one ever to be taken lightly, wrote to the Assembly. "Communication 89-4" was his appeal to the Assembly to: return certain control to the Office of the General Assembly; to more formally establish COGA as an elected body rather than a more *ad hoc* group; and return to a pre-reunion structural style.

This request could easily be dismissed as a weapon in a power struggle, but there is a difference between the church as an ecclesiastical and a programmatic entity that seemed worth preserving, or at least worth fighting about. The General Assembly committee considered Dr. Andrews' letter along with the request from the less powerful COGA and recommended that this concern be added to the assignment to the "to be born" Nature of the Church study.

Then there was an Overture from the Presbytery of John Calvin. Interestingly enough, the action taken by the Assembly on the Overture was to refer the matter to the Advisory Committee on the Constitution – that is, to defer action. But in review it is clear that it was the substance of the Overture from John Calvin that became the "shopping list" of issues that came to be the agenda of this special committee. Here is Overture 89-58:

Overture 89-58 On Appointing a Special Committee to Review Present Form of Government, from the Presbytery of John Calvin

In 1983 the Presbyterian Church in the United States and the United Presbyterian Church in the United States of America adopted The Plan for Reunion. An integral part of The Plan for Reunion was a new Constitution. One part of the Constitution is the Form of Government. Since its adoption, there have been over 250 documents. (sic. presumably a count of proposed amendments and changes)

Whereas, these numerous changes in the Form of Government have resulted in inconsistencies and contradictions within the Form of Government and between it and the Directory of Worship and the Rules of Discipline; and

Whereas, these inconsistencies and contradictions have created problems in interpretation often leading to seeking the advice of the Advisory Committee on the Constitution, whose recommendations must be confirmed by the General Assembly before becoming official, or to reliance on the judicial process of the church; and

Whereas, such delay has lead (sic.) many of the governing bodies either to ignore the Form of Government or to interpret it differently than other governing bodies, thus leading to confusion, conflict and to a rising congregationalism in the Presbyterian Church (U.S.A.); and

Whereas, there have been a number of amendments to the Form of Government which are legislative, administrative or advisory rather than constitutional; therefore, be it

Resolved, That the Presbytery of John Calvin overture the 201st General Assembly (1989) to appoint a special committee for the purpose of reviewing the present Form of Government and recommending proposed changes to the General Assembly after careful study and consultation with appropriate groups or persons and, if deemed necessary, to propose a manual of procedures for governing bodies to the 203rd General Assembly (1991).

When all was said and done a Special Committee on the Nature of the Church and the Practice of Governance (the "its" got lost somewhere along the way) was formed. It was to be made up of persons chosen by the General Assembly Nominating Committee. The directions to the Nominating Committee were not mandated in the action; however, the guidelines suggested by the Program Committee in its request were highly articulated.
"(A) group of 15 representative of a complex of criteria, such as: representatives of both the Theology and Worship Ministry Unit, the Program Committee; persons of theological, sexual, ethnic, cultural and geographic diversity; persons familiar with biblically and historically relevant material; persons with considerable experience and expertise in governance, including at least one with middle governing body (Synod or Presbytery) service; at least one pastor of church over 1000 members and one pastor of church under 200 members, an elder with over 10 yrs experience serving in higher governing bodies and an elder who has served only on a local session."

What the charge to the committee asked it to produce:

an outline of the biblical data regarding both the nature of the church and the concept of governance;

an overview of the statements in the Book of Confessions and the Book of Order regarding the church and its governance, including an analysis of any development or change in our constitutional commitments in this century;

a review of the history of understandings of the church and its governance in American Presbyterianism and in Reformed predecessor bodies;

a survey of views of present members and office bearers and staff in the church;

a comparison of traditional and current Reformed and Presbyterian concepts with those current in ecumenical discussion.

Further, the request indicated a number of current issues of concern to reflect upon:

Theological, ecclesiastical and governance implications of the changes in structure and design of the last two decades.

The effect of the increase in size of presbyteries and synods with consequent changes in their styles, roles and responsibilities with the life of the whole church.

The movement, of decision-making in many presbyteries and synods to their councils with review by the governing body after the decision has taken effect.

The growing use of decision-making styles and procedures which reflect organizational theories which may not reflect Presbyterian principles of governance.

The changes, and resultant confusion, in the roles, responsibility, and relationships of moderators, stated clerks, executives, and other program officers; particularly in light of the COCU [Consultation On Church Union, or perhaps by that time it had already altered its name but not its initials], and other ecumenical conversations.

The presence of distinct experiences and practice of governance emerging from the different racial and ethnic communities within our PCUSA.

The spread of special interest groups (including Chapter IX organizations), some of which hold widely differing views of the nature of the church and the purpose of its structures.

The regular raising of questions about the frequency, style, time and place of meetings of the General Assembly.

The question raised by the authorization of celebration of the Sacraments delegated governing bodies to its councils (including the GAC) and less inclusive governing bodies authorizing celebrations by the more inclusive or their agencies.

And so was born a special committee to study "The Nature of the Church and the Practice of Governance". Three strands of concern came together as the call to a major study and reflection on just who we see ourselves to be as a manifestation of the Body of Christ. The Special Committee met several times each year and at each intervening Assembly reported on its progress. The final report was presented to the General Assembly in 1993 (available at www.pcusa.org/oga, in the publication section). Like so many reports, most of the recommendations were received graciously and referred to another body or merely accepted with a smile and a nod.

Over the years many of the changes sought and recommended were dealt with. The initial concern focused on the entire Book of Order. In the 1990's both the Rules of Discipline and (what is now) the Directory for Worship received comprehensive revision. Indeed, another revision of the Directory for Worship is now being contemplated. Biennial Assembly meetings are now our practice and an elected COGA has been in place for a long time and seems "traditional". The revision of the Form of Government took twenty years. Early attempts were unsuccessful. Substantial revision of one chapter (Chapter 14) was approved in 2006. A four year effort to revise followed. How the matter evolved and continues to be an issue is where we go from here.

[1] The material in this chapter relies in equal parts on my own recollection of events and on a review of the Minutes of the General Assembly. I have not given page and item references for the material from the Minutes but they can be easily traced through the index.

[2] References to the report of the Special Committee on the Nature of the Church and the Practice of Governance are numerous in the pages that follow. I have reduced quoted excerpts to a minimum. The full report (without recommendations that were not approved) is available at www.pcusa.org/oga in the "publications' section.

Chapter Two: The Committee seeks to define the current situation

Preface[1]

Anyone who becomes a member of the PC(USA) is also a member of the one holy catholic and apostolic church. Each is a member of that church by baptism with water in the name of the triune God, and a confirmed member of the PC(USA) by personal profession of faith in Jesus Christ as Savior and Lord (see, Book of Order, G-5.0101)

That is the opening paragraph of the Preface to the report of the committee on The Nature of the Church and the Practice of Governance, 1993. While the reference is to G-5.0101, this is not a direct quotation. The then existing text began with God's incarnation in Jesus Christ an action out of which our membership flows. This opening assertion in the committee report creates a much more "instrumental" understanding. The point of beginning is the effect of becoming a member, that is, coming into the community of the Church through baptism. But the action of the Church in baptism and receiving a (subsequent) profession creates membership. That the Church is the instrument of Christ is a particular understanding of the Church.

Aspects of how we come to be and what it means to be a member of the Presbyterian Church (U.S.A.) are reflected in both the Constitutional and the Preface statements. Our understanding of "Church" is rooted in the incarnation. The Westminster Confession (XXV) defines the Church as all those who profess. The same tradition is traced back to and through Nicea, where the notion of one, holy, catholic, and apostolic (and the commas matter for each adjective is distinct in its own right) makes its foundational claim. The understanding that God's Providence calls the Church out of the world to be the Body of Christ and the more instrumental notion that the Church originates in our profession ("You are the Christ") are both firmly planted in our heritage.

Thoughtful folk have long wrestled with the meaning of membership. In a discussion that easily connects to the earliest considerations between infant baptism (as a sign of belonging to a community) and adult believer baptism (as reflecting a mature acknowledgement of God's action in Jesus Christ) just when one becomes a "member" and what that membership means have been lively topics of concern. In the years after World War II, growing out of the neo-orthodox theology so prominent in that era, baptism took on a more expansive and central meaning among "our kind" of Protestants in relation to our use of the term "member".

---

[1] I will use FOG reference numbers as current at the time of the reference. I trust the reader will be able to keep the dates and various changes in mind as we go along.

Prior to the middle of the last century, when Presbyterians talked about members we spoke of "communicant members". Members were those who had been admitted to the Lord's Table. One did not take the bread and the cup casually. The Directory for Worship specified that sermons prior to communion Sundays instruct the hearers on the meaning of the sacrament. Tokens were given out (well into the twentieth century in some congregations) that entitled the bearer to approach the table as one prepared. To be a follower of Jesus Christ, to be called into community, to bear upon oneself the joy and obligation to witness to his life death and resurrection is a result of baptism and falls equally on all baptized persons.

While the theological assertions about baptism are quite valid, this emphasis on the meaning of membership being tied directly to baptism resulted in two ways of looking at membership, virtually two categories. There is membership in the broad sense of all who have received baptism. This understanding is clearly demonstrated in the Constitutional change enacted in the early 1970s that permitted children being prepared for membership to participate at the Lord's Table. Yet old understandings change slowly as evidence by the use of the term "confirmed member" in the Preface to the Nature of the Church study, a term comfortable and filled with meaning for the authors, but one that does not exist in the Constitution, which speaks only of an "active member".

The meaning of membership becomes then a central question in the consideration of how it is we choose to be church. "Who is a member of our congregation?" is a vital question that is constantly before each session. "Who is a member of the Presbytery?" is a question fundamental to so much of the debate that has stressed the community for two generations. It is for those who are members that we write Constitutions and it is for members that we revise them.

The core of our understanding of the call of Jesus Christ is that we are to follow. Before we know all that following involves; when we are still seated far off under the shade of a tree; Jesus calls and we respond. Following comes first. (John 1:43ff) The current text of the Form of Government (G-5.0101a) has it right. God, incarnate in Jesus calls us and we respond in activity based in faith in Jesus as Savior and acceptance that he is Lord of our life. Baptism is the under-girding symbol, but it is our response to the invitation that "members" us. It is for that reason that the term we use to describe an awareness of membership in Christ's Church is the term "Active Member".

Unfortunately, the bulk of our discussion around this topic speaks in mechanistic terms. Thinking of our polity, the reality is that we are more concerned with the behavior of "adults" in community than of all to whom Christ came. Certainly one of the challenges to within our Form of Government is to describe membership as something that is the result of baptism whenever that may occur. The current Form of Government (G-1.0304) places the matter in the very beginning.

Membership in the Church of Jesus Christ is a joy and a privilege. It is also a commitment to participate in Christ's mission. A faithful member bears witness to God's love and grace and promises to be involved responsibly in the ministry of Christ's Church. Such involvement includes:

There follows a list of eleven forms of action descriptive of the lifestyle of a Jesus-follower, actions that mark a person as a member. The central understanding we carry about membership in the Church and in a church is that members are those who do member things. Such things are observable, they are reportable. Some were concerned that the category of "Inactive Member" was eliminated from the Constitution. The simple response to the concern is, "Inactive Member is an oxymoron." If member is what one does, then one who is not doing is not a member.

What are we to do with those folk who do not, for some measured period of time, fulfill the expectations of activity that describe members? I'm reminded that at one point in Jesus' ministry he laid some heavy expectations about and many "ceased from following him" (John 6:66). Can it be as clear as saying that we either follow or we don't?

Historically, we have understood that accepting the implication of our baptism was to accept a sacred obligation. The failure to fulfill that obligation was a betrayal of a vow and was subject to discipline in the court of the church. Here is the language of the Book of Discipline, of the UPCUSA, Chapter VII, section 4, 1965-1966 edition:

Any resident church member who shall persistently absent himself from the ordinances of the church for two years in a manner to be regarded as a serious injury to the cause of religion may, after diligent effort has been made by the session to restore him to active fulfillment of his membership, and he has been duly notified of its intention, be suspended from the communion of the Church until he shall satisfy the session of the propriety of his restoration.

The heading of that chapter was, "Of Cases Without Full Judicial Process". It included the erasure of names at the person's request, the demitting of a minister against whom no charges were pending and non-resident members who could not be located or persuaded to seek transfer. The underlying assumption here is perfectly clear. Being received into the church as a member is to have undertaken an obligation of following Jesus that is defined by the church. Failure to follow is a matter of utmost seriousness. Failed followers are an embarrassment to the Gospel. Under those circumstances, maintaining a list of those who had been suspended from the communion was important. The Roll of Suspended Members, with the date and circumstances of their suspension was required.

Now, with time, we have found the notion of "judicial process" (even if it was more casually viewed than requiring a full "trial" – and even if with reunion we stopped calling the "courts of the church" judicatories) harsh and unfriendly. Gradually these former cases without full process have moved from the Rules of Discipline over into the Form of Government. And we found "suspension" to be an undesirable concept. Inactivity seemed more appropriate. So the suspended roll became an inactive roll.

Of course our responsibility as a community of faith is to proclaim the good news in word and deed to all. So even those who no longer fall within the community of the active are entitled to hear and receive. Jesus himself did not deny saving news to those outside the bounds of his community, even the dogs are allowed to share in the crumbs that fall from the table. (Matthew 15:26-28) A careful reading of the Form of Government ensures that anyone, member or non, is welcome to share in the life and joys of the gospel. All who have received baptism and been a member of a church are welcome to the sacraments. Only holding office and voting in the congregation are denied to inactive and non-members, two categories who are alike in every respect.

Coming Together, Falling Apart

We are in the early '90s and constitutionally the 8 years since Reunion have seen a flurry of amendments. In addition, office relocation along with a seemingly constant whirlpool of administrative and structural changes, has enveloped us in wonderment as to what we have gotten ourselves into. Much of the foment and ferment that took place between 1983 and the call for the study on the Nature of the Church and the Practice of Governance found its roots in the soil of a Book of Order blending not only north and south but new material from the workings of the reunion committee itself. Still, hostility between north and south was allowed to fester and grow because we were ignorant of each other and the agendas brought by the planners. Don't get me wrong, reunion needed to happen. My idealist side agrees with the argument at the time that we were making witness to fulfilling Christ's prayer that all may be one. Still, we executed a more radical shift in 1983 than most of us realized at the time.

The opening section of the Nature of the Church and the Practice of Governance report is an attempt to describe "The Current Situation"

The denomination is "fragmented and uncertain", the report asserted, continuing, "A key question is: How does our history....inform us today? Then followed this phrase, "On the other hand, in what ways are we -- and perhaps all Christian bodies -- different denominations than we have ever been before, thus making the lessons of Presbyterian history less applicable? Our historically participative denominational life is fragmented by increasing delegation to smaller groups of people, while decreasing broad participation, knowledge, and care about denominational decisions."

Stop right there (for the moment):

What do we mean by "participation" in a denomination? Over the 40 years of my ministry two words/concepts have been used as motto/metaphor/litmus with a limited degree of analysis. Those two words are "connectionalism" and "congregationalism". They are tossed into all kinds of discussions as a trump card, a card that either asserts the righteousness of the speaker's position (as in, "After all, we are a connectional church!") or the derelict position of the other side (as in "If we were to do that it would be just one more evidence of creeping congregationalism!").

Of course both sides can be correct. On the one hand we assert that the church is "One". We vow to support the "Unity" of the church. We ordain our leaders "as an act of the WHOLE church". On the other hand, at the same time we vest original jurisdiction away from the center; in fact, in two places, and in two places least likely to reflect the will of the "whole". The ultimate authority to initiate and to approve rests in the session of a particular congregation and in a particular geographical presbytery. This sets us up for a degree of un-resolvable ambiguity. For us, if there is to be any "centralized" authority and definable "unity" we must rely upon administrative review and judicial process. In any discussion of the Form of Government and particularly when folk speak with veiled threat of a dreaded "local option"; I think it could be helpful to acknowledge that the blessings of connectionalism and the curse of congregationalism are not helpful concepts.

Our history informs us that in the American experience of Presbyterianism the fundamental core of the life of faith resides, first and foremost, in a gathering of believers, called by God and seeking to be faithful followers. We call those gatherings a "congregation". Its leaders (the 'elders', Ruling and Teaching, the latter approved by a presbytery) have lent spiritual and fiscal support to the cause of Christ through whatever means and structures seemed best. When most of what seemed best was denominationally defined, we were "connected"; when the free market prevailed we were "fragmented". In reality we were, and are, and likely always will be, some of both and a lot of neither.

"Polity" and "Mission" May Not Mean What They Used To Mean

"The focus of the Form of Government shall be on providing leadership for local congregations as missional communities." (Minutes of the General Assembly 2006 -assignment to the FOG Task Force)

I will be right up front on this: I trust the Spirit to work what is best for the church through the deliberations and actions of the General Assembly. But I do not always think that the Spirit's Vocabulary Adviser is particularly effective. "Missional" was not the first word I might have invented, or, as others invented it, chosen to use. But it was in the charge to revise the FOG.

To the best of my recollection (and minimal research) it was Emil Brunner who said something to the effect of "the church exists for (or by) mission as a fire exists by burning". That bumper-sticker sized ecclesiology was immensely popular in the late 1960s. But the search for words and phrases to capture the complexity and purpose of the Church of Jesus Christ is eternal.

In the American experience (for we must start somewhere), surely the debates of the 1830s were significant. The complex struggle with the church's civic involvement raged around efforts related to the abolition of slavery. The internal debates on ordination wrestled with whether persons could be ordained to ministries other than a pastoral ministry. Both of these were debates about the nature of the church. There are book-length treatments tracing how these "sides" have carried on this discussion for nigh on 200 years.

Not surprisingly the Nature of the Church and the Practice of Governance report saw the discussion as central to the "current situation" in 1993. *"Since 1972, our emphasis on labeling all church activity as "mission" has genuinely blurred the concepts and challenges of choosing mission priorities for all levels of the church's life. Governing body councils ... have often been empowered by or assumed power for a governing body, thus decreasing ownership in both process and outcome"*

Across the years, when the word "mission" is used in this debate, its meaning has suffered. Why are we here? What are we to do? or, What is Christ's/The/our mission? The word carries too much meaning to be used as an adjective for anything. Yet the current word of the day is "missional" - adjectivally trivializing. To faithfully follow the mandate, the Task Force to Revise the Form of Government looked to Dr. Darrell Guder who has written extensively in these terms. Also sustenance was found in the work of Jurgen Moltman. The current text understands the church in Moltman's perspective. In summary: *"What we must learn is not that the Church has a mission, but the very reverse: that the mission of Christ creates its own Church"* [cited by Dr. Paul Hooker: 'What is Missional Ecclesiology' - prepared for the Task Force].

Consideration of mission has a long history. A group of pious and energetic young men from Williams College huddled in a haystack during a rainstorm one evening in 1806. The result of their prayers is widely believed to be genesis of the great American missionary enterprise of the 19th and early 20th centuries. Mission "Boards", supported by all sorts of congregations and individuals flourished. During the post Civil War period many of these autonomous boards were taken into the formal structures of the denominations, including the Presbyterian Church in the U.S.A. (and, I presume the Presbyterian Church in the United States, although my knowledge is pretty much limited to the former "northern stream.)

The best way to describe the relationship was one of semi-autonomy. Each year the General Assembly would elect members to serve on the "boards" and receive reports of their "work". I doubt that anyone would have suggested that these boards and agencies were engaged in anything other than the "mission work" of the Presbyterian Church. I doubt that any members of the boards or staff of these groups would think themselves as having any great independence from the life and work of the whole church. Still, they were separated in a real sense and remained self-perpetuating in many senses of the word.

The evangelistic missionary work of the nineteenth century bore fruit. In areas of our own country where the need for witness was great "Homeland" or "National" missionaries served in starting churches, schools and hospitals. Presbyterian congregations in other lands were formed under missionary leadership. These congregations ultimately were constituted as "synods" of our denomination and related to the General Assembly in ways similar to those within our borders. Over time these overseas Synods morphed into indigenous churches. Over time they became partners in work and worship and we became resource people. The effect of how mission work (particularly overseas) changed has recently been well documented in a book by Sunquist and Becker, A History of Presbyterian Missions: 1944-2007.

As a child in the church in the years after World War II it was clear to me what "mission" was and who the "missionaries" were. A young man from the Indian sub-continent spent a night in our home on some itineration or other. An African-American woman working for one of the racial-ethnic institutions was a guest at my family's table. I knew that Missionaries were those who went somewhere away from their home to do some work in the name of Jesus. My own seminary intern year was as pastor to a new church development that was struggling for survival. It was a "missionary" effort and was funded by the Board of Church Extension of the Presbytery, the board that cared for the mission of the Presbytery. My first call after ordination was to an urban ministry combining congregational worship and community outreach. My salary came from "mission dollars".

Polity made mission possible. Polity allowed mission to happen. No one felt the need to speak of "polity" and "mission" in the same sentence, both were in the air we breathed.

Yes, everyone knew what mission work was and everyone knew that we were a missionary denomination, reaching out wherever there was need in the name of Jesus Christ. The people in the pews understood missions. As Sunquist and Becker phrase it, the missionaries were honored "*as the supreme examples of Christian service, respected and appreciated by the people among whom they worked ... they responded to God's call and left their home countries to be witnesses for Jesus Christ.*" (p. 76)

But there was an important polity distinction that was beginning to blur. Up until the 1970's the judicatories/courts of the church (lately called 'governing bodies') existed primarily, if not exclusively, to do ecclesiastical business. Sessions and presbyteries were "seats of original jurisdiction". Synods and the General Assembly were populated by (indeed, in the American experience they were creations of) the presbyteries for the purpose of administrative review and judicial appeal. The governing structures existed to govern, not to provide program. As a reminder, even the "Sunday School Movement" began as an evangelistic tool, a para-church organization, and in many congregations had a separate structure and financial reality apart from the session.

The "mission work" was separate from ecclesial business. Particular presbyteries and synods might have some mission programs of their own. A few large urban presbyteries were at the vanguard of establishing programs for their setting and established "special relationships" with the national boards for funding and control. But the General Assembly still related to the various boards in a review and oversight manner. The boards themselves initiated and administered THEIR program. (Beyond foreign and national missions there was also a Board of Christian Education, a Department of Ministerial Relations, a Board of Pensions, and likely a few more if I went digging around in the old minutes) Review by the General Assembly was not control. Receiving a report was not directing a program. Funds were solicited by the boards and agencies directly from sessions. Work was determined and funding distributed from the boards and not from "the General Assembly". The only funds collected by the General Assembly as the General Assembly were the *per capita* assessments on the presbyteries, funds strictly to run the meetings of the Assembly itself and maintain the records of the Stated Clerk. They were called "essential ecclesiastical expenses".

Into the 1950's a common pattern placed staff members of these national boards in the offices of the Synod by mutual agreement and with joint oversight of work. These staff people worked with presbytery and session leadership to interpret the work and direct the flow of benevolent dollars to the national boards.

Then things changed. By the mid-twentieth century notions of the "corporate church" were growing rapidly and efficient administration came to be highly valued. Vertically integrated administration of work was coming to the forefront. And within our Presbyterian family another movement was afoot. A strong effort was made to unite three main branches of the reformed community. Most know that the union of the United Presbyterian Church in North America and the Presbyterian Church in the United States of America that took place in 1958 was designed to include the Presbyterian Church in the United States as well. Work to bring about this union had begun shortly after World War II. Only with the votes of the presbyteries on the plan itself did the presbyteries of the PCUS reject reunion.

What is less well remembered is that within this plan was a fully developed expectation (as early as 1955) to create in the reunited denomination "regional synods". These large synods, comprised of expanded presbyteries, would be staffed with people jointly approved by the General Assembly and the Synod councils. The "staff" of the Synod would be comprised of all ecclesiastical, administrative and programmatic personnel serving within the Synod and of the presbyteries within its bounds. A vertically integrated program of mission (funded by the Boards) would unite and integrate the benevolent/mission work of the church. Of course the union did not happen and those who sought such administrative efficiency (while I can be cynical, I will not accuse anyone of seeking increased power and control) were put off for a time, but not deterred.

In May of 1963, the 175th General Assembly, meeting in Des Moines, Iowa appointed a special committee of nine to *"(A) Examine the possibility of our churches moving toward the establishment of regional synods; and (B) Consider the problems of administration at all judicatory levels in any possible restructuring of the synods of the Church"* The final report was to be submitted in 1966. In the following years the committee reports spelled out in great detail the way in which administration of the work of the church would take place at all levels. It was argued that a new structure was needed for this newly enlarged denomination. The report was approved in 1966 and the committee was expanded to design implementation strategies.

In 1969 the General Assembly received the final report of the "Special Committee on Regional Synods and Church Administration". The report was presented to the Assembly as Overture H. It went by that name until the committee charged with implementing its recommendations titled their report a "Design for Mission". In 1972 approval made this design our structure and process for doing missions.

For this to happen little needed to change from a polity perspective. No foundational understandings needed to be altered. But it changed in the way we saw ourselves. Now we saw ourselves primarily in programmatic rather than ecclesiastical terms. Executive/Administrative staff supplanted ecclesiastical officers as the focal points of activity. The ways in which this worked itself out has had a profound effect across the years.

The primary real change was "at the top". (again, I am referencing only the "northern stream") The semi-autonomous boards and agencies were radically re-cast. All the work that had previously been reviewed by the General Assembly now became, in a way, the work of the General Assembly. The General Assembly Mission Council (UPCUSA) and the General Assembly Mission Board (PCUS) each were coordinating bodies that had oversight of all work, influenced all budgets, and had implied supervision of all staff. (a note: the Board of Pensions and the Presbyterian Foundation retained their former status.) All the dollars (in the "northern stream") that had previously flowed to the boards was assumed now to flow to the General Assembly. Allocation and authorization, formerly "negotiated" among somewhat independent groups were now bargained and bartered within the formerly ecclesiastical structures. There is nothing particularly good or bad about that shift. But there is no question that it represented a major alteration in thinking and practice.

That "shift" is where the polity comes to be altered by the program. The staffing model that was normative in the Design for Mission (there were exceptions) was that of the 1955 plan. Synod staff persons were jointly put in place by the General Assembly and the Synod councils. Presbytery staff persons were similarly jointly agreed to (although I confess that wasn't how I heard it 'on the ground' at the time. What I recall hearing was that presbytery staff people were fully Synod staff people assigned by the Synod, at the Synod's discretion. For the moment I will rely on the printed record of the General Assembly Minutes and say it was mutually agreed upon.)

The flow of dollars was similarly the result of negotiation. Tri-level budgeting consultations were held each year. Representatives came together, each presenting the dollars needed to carry out their governing body's mission program envisioned for the coming year. The dollars available were projected, haggled over, and agreed to. The history of just how this system evolved and ultimately collapsed will need to be the subject of some other historical research, but the seeds of its failure were present from the creation. By 1974-75 there was already a budgeting shortfall of major proportions at the national level. The money that had formerly flowed to the boards did not flow to the GAMC as predicted. Whether it was poor planning or inadequate interpretation, within three years staff was being laid-off and programs cut.

But it was at the presbytery level that things shifted most dramatically. (Again, with exceptions) Prior to this re-organization, presbyteries were almost solely ecclesiastical entities. They were smaller (with urban exceptions) and more concerned with the care and keeping of ministers and congregations. Most had no full-time staff and likely compensated only a pastor in a small congregation to serve as Stated Clerk. Suddenly each presbytery had an "Executive" with an office and, at the very least, a secretary. Work that had been done by volunteers now was the work of "professionals". In the area of mission and outreach such staffing was but an extension of former patterns.

Very quickly however, these "Executives" also provided direct service in the ecclesiastical areas of the presbytery's life. This was something new. While they may well have been knowledgeable and also ordained as either elders or ministers, bearing office was not a requirement for employment. In contrast, those who serve the church in ordered ministries are called by a congregation or to serve in a ministry validated by a presbytery. Such persons are "under discipline" and their work falls directly under the jurisdiction of the church through its Constitutional provisions of administrative and judicial review. These new Executive staff members were more often seen as "hirelings" and their work overseen by a personnel process as employees who served at the will of the council (or jointly by councils).

Very quickly provisions were written into the Constitution to "bless" and legitimate this new creature, but the integration, fusion, and/or blending of the ecclesiastical and programmatic functions of leadership in the church that flowed up and down a vertical line, gave an entirely new organizational image to the church, without re-forming the foundational understandings that original jurisdiction resided in the presbytery and the session.

Before I drift too far, I must poke myself to remember that this "thought string" began with the directive to the Form of Government Task Force to create a more "missional polity". Back in 1972 when the Design for Mission re-shaped the denomination the role/relationship of mission was also central. Brunner's motto "The church exists by mission as fire exists by burning" evolved into a common by-line explaining the new form of church life. Reorganization would follow the claim that "Everything the Church Does Is Its Mission." The idea that God's mission creates the Church has been stood upon its head! Instrumentalism has triumphed.

The new structure reflected a vertical integration. The concept was that dollars and mission projects/objectives were to flow upwards while authorization and funding flowed downward to the point closest to the location of mission need. Rather than a centralized entity defining, directing and controlling mission, mission was to be designed and implemented locally, that is at the *locus* of the need, but with authorization and funding coming "from above".

This is not the venue to explore all the implications of that model or to seek to determine the ways in which it did and did not work out as planned. I do not want to give the impression that the intentions or integrity of the elected representatives who worked to design and oversee this transformation of the church were anything but honorable. If there were conspiracies to violate our understandings as a denomination I am unaware of them. I also do not claim to criticize the intent of those who sought to implement the structures and policies that were approved by the General Assembly. What I put down are the perceptions of a presbytery level staff person and parish pastor. That I may not have correctly perceived the intent or full ramifications of policy is not beside the point but also can no longer be corrected.

Two observations are relevant to how we see our current situation:

1. When the design and the implementation of the work of mission was placed in the same venue as the source of the funding, the General Assembly role in designing and approving mission activity became increasingly irrelevant to the pastors and the people. If the needs we have right here close to home are as important as the work elsewhere, folk reasoned, why should we send money up the line and then have to ask permission to do the work we have already determined is important? There are good arguments against that line of reasoning, but being Calvinists we know that self-serving will trump collegiality every time.

2. If everything the church does is its mission, then it became increasingly difficult to define any particular needs/projects that were more valuable or more appropriate than any other. In a most bizarre twist of reality, it made a certain degree of sense to argue that providing toilet paper in the bathrooms at the presbytery office was as important as providing inoculating serum for orphan children in far-off Africa. Of course that is absurd, but the reality was that there were only so many dollars and if we could not fund the local program effectively, how could we raise the awareness and funds to support the program of the whole church.

One further observation on the effects of the 1972 reorganization (again, I'm familiar only with the former northern church). Prior to this reorganization the per capita funds that were assessed were narrowly defined as funding "essential ecclesiastical expense". At the presbytery level, perhaps a stated clerk, a secretary, some mileage reimbursement, etc. At the level of the GA it primarily covered the office of the Stated Clerk and the meetings of the Assembly. These assessments may have been burdensome, but they were seen as reasonable.

The new plan assumed that all the money formerly spent on the staff and field staff of the various boards would continue to flow upward. So, this former stream of mission dollars, now being funneled back down would fund staff people, who were officially working for synods and presbyteries. The concept was known as "circulating funds". Two things happened, both of them bad. The dollars stopped flowing upward, even as the commitment to send mission dollars down to support staff was still in place. This cut into money available for work at the GA level. When this pattern was determined to be irreversible the understandings were changed and presbyteries began to keep more of their mission dollars "at home" so as to continue the support of the staff mandated by the reorganization but now determined to be invaluable.

The second result of circulating funds was the perception that a conversion of dollars took place, by which money offered to the church as "mission dollars" or "benevolence offerings" changed into money that paid expenses previously viewed as ecclesiastical expenses. The perception was unleashed that taking care of our presbytery's needs was described as "mission". We wanted the work to be done; we loved our presbytery staff; we needed the professionalism they brought to a declining volunteer pool; but toilet paper in the presbytery office was NOT MISSION! Many tried to shift more of these functions into per capita, but that increased the assessment to a level more obviously burdensome and in the mind of many pastors and pew-sitters, definitely unreasonable.

These are but some of the aspects of "the current situation" described by the committee in 1993 that continue to be with us today.

Toward a Missional Polity

As I understand the use of the word, *missional*, it seeks to speak of the call of Christ to preach good news to a world that is far different than the world in which our ancestors first shaped the great "missionary movement" of the nineteenth century. We are different, but more importantly, the world is different. Darrell Guder in his The Continuing Conversion of the Church, speaks of our traditional desire to control not only how the gospel is proclaimed but also the results of that proclamation. In other words, when the gospel is faithfully proclaimed, the result will be recognizable. If what we see is not what we expect, then the proclamation was faulty or ineffective. Guder's view is that in our contemporary reality the function and purpose of proclamation is translation. He asserts that the "gospel is fundamentally not controllable. It unsettles us to discover that faithfulness to Christ can, in cultures different from ours, look different from the patterns we have evolved. ... mission as translation means that the apostolic ministry of witness takes place in a plurality of cultural forms. None of them is normative for the others. But they are all essential to each other as mutual affirmation, correction, and challenge." [p.90ff]

Later, beginning with the familiar dictum, "*Ecclesia reformata secundum verbi Dei semper reformanda* (the church once reformed is always in the process of being reformed according to the Word of God.)" he continues, "There is a tendency to solve problems by reorganization. What I have tried to make clear is that the church's crisis is one of fundamental vocation, of calling to God's mission, of being, doing and saying witness in faithfulness to Jesus Christ, the Lord. Our missional challenge is a crisis of faith and spirit, and it will be met only through conversion...."[p.150]

When the Task Force began its work we shared Guder's writings as part of the foundation for our early discussion. If we were to re-shape our polity in light of missional theology, what effect would that theology have? I believe the revision, and thus the FOG, is faithful to the task and not inconsistent with that theology. The most dramatic change is that sessions and presbyteries will be invited (no, perhaps I should just flat-out say, required) to reflect and act on how our foundational understandings of what it means to be Presbyterian leads us to respond to Christ's invitation as each body encounters its own unique situation in the world.

The apostle Paul wrote to the Corinthians: "For if I do this of my own will, I have a reward; but if not of my own will, I am entrusted with a commission. What then is my reward? Just this: that in my proclamation I may make the gospel free of charge, so as not to make full use of my rights in the gospel. For though I am free with respect to all, I have made myself a slave to all, so that I might win more of them. ... I do it all for the sake of the gospel, so that I may share in its blessings. [1 Corinthians 9:17-19;23]

Stanley Hauerwas has written: "(T)he way the church must always respond to the challenge of our polity is to be herself. This does not involve a rejection of the world, or a withdrawal from the world; rather it is a reminder that the church must serve the world on her own terms. We must be faithful in our own way, even if the world understands such faithfulness as disloyalty. "[A Community of Character, p.85]

Chapter Three: What the Committee Agreed On

The Nature of the Church and the Practice of Governance Report of 1993 concludes its understanding of "The Current Situation" with these words: "Although we as a committee were often far from unanimous about particular recommendations, we came to have consensus around certain things:" What follows is a bullet-point listing of the committee's observations. Reading the list is as good as reading today's news.

Item # 1

"The denomination is at a major turning point. The direction in which it turns will affect its institutional and mission future, its membership, and its vitality."

At what point in the sea journey, or, at which moment in time was the captain of the Titanic in a position to turn? Or, stated in the negative, at what point was it too late? In my life time the denomination has come to many decision points and made major turns. Consequences were not always anticipated and collateral results often not addressed.

- The 1958 merger (in its incompleteness that necessitated 1983 reunion).

- The three major studies on what we mean by ordination and the ever strengthened assertion that ministry (Unfortunately, the word we commonly use to describe ordered ministry, particularly that of a Teaching Elder in a congregation.) is the result of baptism and bears on all believers.

- The subsequent admission of baptized children to the Lord's Table, thus eliminating the term "Communicant" as our primary definer of membership in a congregation.

- The addition of categories of inclusiveness and diversity as foundational "marks" of the Church equivalent to the historic marks of Nicea, Knox, and Calvin.

To my eye aspects of that list remain as open questions before us. Are we not always at a turning point? And, whether we turn or not, do we not trust God's Spirit to guide the Church? The folk back in 1993 believed that we needed to turn. The current Book of Order now reflects that turning and is the outgrowth of portions of their conclusion. Do these new realities place our framework of governance closer to how we actually govern and the contemporary reality of our life together?

Items # 2 & 3

"People of genuine faith in the PC(USA) have very different perceptions about the present, the past, and the future." [THUS] "A distinctly Presbyterian faith is obscured in the current life of the denomination in light of its pluralism of belief and participation of persons from various denominational backgrounds."

Yup, that's sure true. And, it likely was true in the 1730's when the Tennent family was setting the church afire; and in the 1830's when the issue of abolition and ordaining evangelists like Charles Finney were being fought over; and in the 1920s when the Scopes trial captured national attention and Harry Emerson Fosdick was being swept upriver to preach in Mr. Rockefeller's chapel.

Why did the Special Committee note these two, seemingly, self-evident observations, and why consider them in discussing the Form of Government?

Every age needs to answer this question for itself, "Can we create a plan and pattern of faithfulness that more adequately presents the good news of Jesus Christ?" If God has no grandchildren this is more than an idle question, it is a positive mandate. Pragmatism alone cannot rule the day. If flexibility and creativity are to be available to the church, then the church requires efforts to refine and re-assert the foundational basis on which we act. In drawing out the Foundational Principles on which governance rests, and collecting them in a separate section, the FOG seeks to make these core principles accessible as a teaching tool. We are a diverse gathering of folk and increasingly a gathering with limited common heritage or historical knowledge. The Task Force claimed as a primary objective the creation of a document suitable for teaching those new to or slightly familiar with our tradition and practice. The Foundations section is a response to this perceived need.

Yet, even the most optimistic one among us knows that simply having a common document will not end the reality of diversity in both belief and practice. James Russell Lowell penned the words, "New occasions teach new duties, time makes ancient good uncouth." The FOG provides to the councils of the church the flexibility to respond while staying close to our foundational common understandings.

Items # 4, # 5 & #6

Distinct characteristics about how Presbyterians have understood faith and order can be found in the current Book of Order, but the Book of Order cannot be the primary unifying document for our denomination in either its practice or its theory;

Lack of understanding of Presbyterianism -- historically and currently -- promotes dependence on future delegation of authority to councils and individuals, and accentuates the Book of Order *as a way to develop uniformity when no other uniformity exists.*

Diversity of opinion about social issues, biblical interpretation, theological positions, and life experience increases a lack of consensus about direction in mission priorities

The part about a lack of understanding is key and, to my eye, pretty obvious. But I don't get the part about "future" dependence since it was clear from the middle of the last century that a bureaucratic/corporate model of authority had already come to the fore. [A NOTE HERE: "councils" used in this sentence of the report refers to the typical "general council" or some such "executive committee" function that was mandated in the then current text. It does NOT refer to the way council is used to describe the governing body of authority in the current FOG.]

That the Book of Order has become our *de facto* unity is a claim regularly made. But, if we are to be a gathering of people whose lives are centered on such a book, the discrete section of foundational principles is even more essential than if we continued to read the book the way most folk would look at guidelines or 'standing rules'.

The next assertion, about diversity of opinion, repeats the thought stated above in item number three on the list. Most of us don't consider diversity of opinion a problem. Certainly it is inevitable in human communities. I doubt there are very many leaders or pew sitters within any of our congregations who would seek to live in a community where there was no diversity of opinion. We have names for such communities (utopias, if we like the opinions and Orwellian dictatorships, if we don't) but few of us would likely enjoy living in them.

Does diversity then become an excuse for a failure to sit down face to face and do the hard work of seeking common ground? In society, the political polarization we see reflects that reality. Political debate on important issues shows us that an unwillingness to flex and bend with and toward others destroys even face-to-face conversation. Does it need to also be so in the church?

If setting apart a clear section of foundational principles; and asserting primary authority and responsibility in the governing councils (presbyteries and sessions) where people of faith have the greatest opportunity to know each other and understand each other's lives, 'face to face'; can bring us together in a shared mission and ministry, then the revision of the FOG will achieve what it was called out to do.

Item # 7

In claiming to value racial ethnic and theological diversities, we choose to manifest those by requiring membership on committees and councils rather than learning the cultural, racial, and theological values we want to incorporate into our denominational life.

This somewhat convoluted confession of valuing institutional placement over faith-filled human engagement opens for us an aspect of our life together that is a major "sticky wicket". Whatever our actual behavior has been, the official denominational position asserts that membership in the church is open to all and based in profession of faith, alone. Those who "bear office"; those who are chosen to "govern/rule" among us; are to be chosen based on a higher standard of qualification. Depth of faith and integrity of practice are the measures that invite the church to call a given member into leadership. However, this item on the special committee's list calls attention to a way of thinking relatively new in our practice.

The evolution that led us to the 1993 report's concern came into focus in parallel with the Civil Rights Movement of the late 1950's and beyond. Sometime between 1956 (Constitution of the Presbyterian Church in the United States of America) and 1965 (Constitution of the United Presbyterian Church in the United States of America) the following paragraph was inserted to clarify just what was meant by "all":

To belong to a church is to belong to a fellowship which must learn to welcome all persons who would hear of God's mercy in Jesus Christ and desire to share in the worship and service of Christ's Church. Each church member must seek the grace for this kind of openness in extending the fellowship of Christ to all such persons in the knowledge that failure to do so, on the basis of color, origin or worldly condition, constitutes a rejection of Christ himself and causes a scandal to the gospel. (1965-1966 Form of Government, VI:3

I have no problem endorsing the conclusion that refusing to accept a person of faith or consider one for office, based on 'color, origin, or worldly condition' is a 'scandal to the gospel.' I believed it then and believe it now. I preached it then and would preach it now. The issue is, of course, that preaching is not the function of a constitutional document. Asserting that all who profess faith are members simply defines a reality that sets the church apart from other organizations whose members share some other trait, practice or belief. While it is fully appropriate and necessary for the church to define what behaviors are acceptable for members, placing lists and descriptors into our constitution starts us down the slippery slope toward creating a manual rather than a constitution.

Then again, this is not new. We were there before. In the 19th century the constitution prohibited (either in the text or in its interpretation) that those who chose to work on the Sabbath for the purpose solely of making gain, or those who produced or sold alcoholic beverages, or those who practiced polygamy could not be ordained to office. So making lists of what members could or couldn't do or be is not foreign to us. However, in the current context attention is focused on the current listing of 'color, origin or worldly condition'.

This listing came over into the Constitution with reunion as (former) G-4.0403. Actually, by 1983 the list had been expanded to: "Persons of all racial ethnic groups, different ages, both sexes, various disabilities, diverse geographical areas, and different theological positions consistent with the Reformed tradition"; and then went on to add "shall be guaranteed full participation and access to representation in the decision making of the Church."

The "scandal" of prejudicial discrimination now has a foundational corrective, a guarantee of participation and access. At the end of the above sentence the reader is referred to G-9.0104ff. Therein stands the procedural mandate to governing bodies to "work" to achieve this guarantee and specifies the make-up of the committee charged with making it happen, the Committee on Representation. This committee is to be made up of "majority male, majority female, racial ethnic male, racial ethnic female (and) youth male and female" members.

I have no objection to the principle or the goal of canceling prejudicial behavior and reflecting the great diversity of our community into the markings of those who lead. But the foundational principle of governance in our tradition rests on those who "bear office" in the church. Leadership and responsibility is vested in presbyters, those called Ruling and Teaching Elders. Over the years roles of leadership fulfilled by church members who are not ordained in service to the deliberative bodies of governance has been contentious. Rulings have gone back and forth. In the latter half of the twentieth century the pendulum of opinion favored opening active leadership to not ordained to one of the ordered ministries.

However, there remained a principled restriction on the committees dealing with ecclesiastical matters; a limitation to only those ordained. In this regard the former provision of a Committee on Representation represented a constitutionally mandated committee in all governing bodies above the session composed in a new and unique fashion and without reference to the ordered ministries. [The provision for a Nominating Committee is also unique, being made up of 1/3 laymen; 1/3 laywomen; and 1/3 ministers - thus leaving elders as optional members and declaring ministers to be a third gender certainly is another unique and unusual innovation that accompanied reunion.]

By 1993 it had become apparent that not every governing body had the capacity to effectively provide for such a committee. (Yes, it is possible that they did not function effectively because they rejected the goal, but enforcement through normal administrative review could do little to correct that.) And, it was becoming apparent to some who looked far enough ahead, that presbyteries could evolve in which there was no one majority population. In pursuit of the goal we were regulating a system guaranteed to produce scofflaws!

This reality has not changed since 1993 and become more evident. In seeking to drop manual material from the FOG the mandated Committee on Representation has been retained (not without objection from the drafting Task Force!) but in a "softer" form.

The Form of Government however is serious in seeking to maintain the strength of our tradition of full inclusivity within our diversity. Consider the following:

Foundations 1.0403

The unity of believers in Christ is reflected in the rich diversity of the Church's membership. In Christ, by the power of the Spirit, God unites persons through baptism regardless of race, ethnicity, age, sex, disability, geography, or theological conviction. There is therefore no place in the life of the Church for discrimination against any person. The Presbyterian Church (U.S.A.) shall guarantee full participation and representation in its worship, governance, and emerging life to all persons or groups within its membership. No member shall be denied participation or representation for any reason other than those stated in this Constitution.

G 2.0401 Election of Ruling Elders and Deacons

Ruling elders and deacons are men and women elected by the congregation from among its members. The nomination and election of ruling elders and deacons shall express the rich diversity of the congregation's membership and shall guarantee participation and inclusiveness (F-1.0403). Ruling elders and deacons shall be nominated by a committee elected by the congregation, drawn from and representative of its membership.

G 3.0103 Participation and Representation

Each council shall develop procedures and mechanisms for promoting and reviewing that body's implementation of the church's commitment to inclusiveness and representation. Councils above the session shall establish by their own rule committees or entities to fulfill...

It's all still there. I know that some feel it is not enough, but our commitment to inclusivity has not wavered.

Item # 8 through # 11

These items frustrate and baffle and I will not quote them even as I acknowledge them for any keeping numerical score.

In them is the usual lament that there is not enough money to do the mission. They nod to its ongoing nature and allege poor management; but the special committee's final leveling of blame falls on the people in the pew who are just not being sufficiently generous. Against these assertions is the reality that giving has continued to rise, it has just not risen upward through the imagined structure of a hierarchy of institutional forms.

Part of the blame for the problem is then laid at the door of membership decline. It is a critical issue, of course, but it is also a dead horse and kicking it does not offer much in the way of change. "Congregationalism" is decried even as the virtue of local empowerment is lauded. Finally, our cherished slogan "Reformed always to be Reformed"(sic) is brought out with the interpretation that we must demonstrate how we are in partnership in God's activity.

There, I've covered four bullet points. I see them as somewhere in the realm of hackneyed, cliché ridden and unhelpful. But you can go read them for yourself if you wish.

Item # 12

"Our concept of representation has changed. While we maintain that ministers and elders serve uninstructed by their constituencies, persons are often selected or appointed to represent certain cultural, racial or theological perspectives in the denomination. Nonordained persons also serve. We have yet to see the long-term consequences, both positive and negative"

This one is pretty significant. To set a context for consideration I put forward a portion of the current text.

F - 3.0202 Governed by Presbyters

This church shall be governed by presbyters, that is, ruling elders and teaching elders. Ruling elders are so named not because they "lord it over" the congregation (Matt. 20:25), but because they are chosen by the congregation to discern and measure its fidelity to the Word of God, and to strengthen and nurture its faith and life. Teaching elders shall be committed in all their work to equipping the people of God for their ministry and witness.

F - 3.0203 Gathered in Councils

These presbyters shall come together in councils in regular gradation.

G - 3.0103 Participation and Representation

The councils of the church shall give full expression to the rich diversity of the church's membership and shall provide for full participation and access to representation in decision-making and employment practices (F-1.0403). In fulfilling this commitment, councils shall give due consideration to both the gifts and requirements for ministry (G-2.0104) and the right of people in congregations and councils to elect their officers (F-3.0106).

Each council shall develop procedures and mechanisms for promoting and reviewing that body's implementation of the church's commitment to inclusiveness and representation. Councils above the session shall establish by their own rule committees or entities to fulfill the following functions: to advise the council regarding the implementation of principles of unity and diversity, to advocate for diversity in leadership, and to consult with the council on the employment of personnel, in accordance with the principles of unity and diversity in F1.0403.

G - 3.0301 Composition and Responsibilities

The presbytery is the council serving as a corporate expression of the church within a certain district and is composed of all the congregations and teaching elders within that district. Teaching elders and ruling elders should be present in numbers as equal as possible. The presbytery shall adopt and communicate to the sessions a plan for determining how many ruling elders each session should elect as commissioners to presbytery. This plan shall require each session to elect at least one commissioner and shall take into consideration the size of congregations as well as a method to fulfill the principles of participation and representation found in F-1.0403 and G-3.0103. Ruling elders elected as officers of the presbytery shall be enrolled as members during the period of their service. A presbytery may provide by its own rule for the enrollment of ruling elders serving as moderators of committees or commissions.

The Nature and Practice folk said: "Our concept of representation has changed." Yup! So let's talk a bit about representation. From the first, ministers (oops, Teaching Elders) maintained membership in a separate body, the presbytery (as they had been 'membered' in the Roman Catholic church when they were the 'agents' of their bishop who was an agent of 'The' bishop who was an agent of Christ the great Head of the Church.). In that separate body care was taken to see to it that congregations were safeguarded from false doctrine and shoddy preaching. "Ruling" elders were invited to sit with the ministers as the governing body for particular congregations. As presbyteries evolved, ruling elders served as representatives from the congregations, seated alongside the minister members. When a vote was taken, ministers and ruling elders each had a vote, but they voted as two different types of "members" in the presbytery. A presbytery was simply a geographical district (defined by some minimum number of congregations within its bounds) and there was no Constitutional concern as to how many of either category of member might be present and eligible to vote.

That summarizes how things functioned well into the twentieth century. The purpose of a presbytery was to safeguard the gospel by seeing to it that ministers who met the test of what it meant to be "Presbyterian" served the congregations within its bounds. This function of guarding congregations has been passed down through the centuries as a principle understanding of why we ordain leaders. We may have abandoned the medieval notion of an indelible change in the person's character that accompanied the "laying on of hands" (which at the time of my ordination in 1970 was still done only by the minister members of the presbytery), but we never abandoned the notion that the special function of ordination to the "gospel ministry" (one of the earlier designations of the office) was to see to the oversight and care, that is the governance of the church.

What did that mean in relation to the composition of a presbytery? For a meeting to happen, a set number of ministers needed to be present and a set number of congregations needed to be represented (a quorum requirement), but congregations were only represented in relation to the pastoral numbers assigned to them. Hence, a "collegiate church" (one with more than one called pastor) was allowed representatives equal to the number of called pastors. On the other hand, a yoked field of more than one congregation served by the same pastor was assigned only one commissioner from all the congregations of the field.

The foundational principles beneath the existence of a presbytery is ecclesiastical responsibility; the care of congregations through the provision of pastoral leadership. Representation, in this context reflects an equal voice and vote among those who bear office, which means minister members and representatives from congregations. The composition of a presbytery as a governing body is made up of two different types of persons, its members and those whose membership reflects their representative authority as ruling elders in congregations overseen by the presbytery.

In the twentieth century the concept evolved to mean that ministers and ruling elders were present in something approximating equal numbers. In rural presbyteries, once each session was entitled to a representative, the balance was skewed toward an excess of ruling elders. In larger, more urban presbyteries more likely it was the other way around. Manual provisions came into the Constitution to mandate that these "imbalances" be rectified.

But there is a second dynamic in the evolution of our understanding of "representative". This came about with the rapid increase in the number of specialized ministries after World War II. As late as the 1970s it was most unusual (virtually unknown) for someone to be ordained to the ministerial office for any service other than a "call" to the pastoral ministry in a parish. Chaplaincy ministries were few and, for the most part, unavailable to anyone without a demonstrated track record of successful parish ministry. There were "minister members" and "session commissioners" comprising the presbytery and the life and work of a worshiping congregation was the common life of them all.

However, with the increase of minister members not related directly to parish ministry and life expectancy leading to a larger number of Honorably Retired members, the values and experiences "represented" in the body came to be more broadly focused than primarily focused on the ecclesiastical business related to congregations. This broadening was further augmented with the reorganizations of the 1970s that drove concern for mission/program down to the presbytery and session level. Now the business of the governing body was increasingly less ecclesiastical and more programmatic (and in many cases more political). Voting blocs and issue-oriented groupings shifted from being concerned primarily with theological differences and into a host of concerns parallel to those in the wider culture.

Constitutional changes responded to this by lifting up diversity as a benchmark for understanding the nature of the church. Our understanding of the representative nature of a governing body shifted from being a reflection of the "church", as it was, toward seeking a more comprehensive reflection of the church as we wished it to be.

Thus, when commissioners were sent to a governing body meeting, directions were given to nominate and elect persons such as to fill certain quotas. Presbyteries were directed by synods to nominate a "racial-ethnic woman elder" for a particular position rather than simply "an elder". Clearly, our understanding of what it means to have a representative form of governance is vastly different than a few generations ago.

The Nature of the Church and Practice of Governance committee wrote: "We have yet to see the long-term consequences, both positive and negative." I would not venture to argue that we have seen those consequences clearly even now. Surely we see a wider vision of the church in our higher governing bodies. That's good in drawing a picture of what we think the Kingdom of God will be like. Still, the overwhelming demographic of our congregations is white and over a certain age. We may wish it to be other. We certainly should work to reach out and make it more reflective of the Kingdom than it is. But, we are who we are and the challenge is to find a way not to leave what we are really like un-represented in our desire to implement a vision of what we wish/hope we might become.

Another factor contributing to a loss of clarity about the foundational pillars of our polity is the dilution of, no, the downright sloppiness we demonstrate in our use of language. I know that the dictionary will give ample support for saying that the words "representative", "delegate" and "commissioner" can, and in certain circumstances do, mean the same thing. So, when someone says "I'm the "representative" from my church to the presbytery meeting." they have said nothing wrong. Nor has the one who says that they are the "delegate" from their presbytery to the General Assembly. Still, both uses are like fingernails on a blackboard to my polity ear. Even more troubling are the Teaching Elders who speak on the floor of a presbytery and introduce themselves as Minister Commissioners or Minister delegates to the presbytery! My colleague and my friend, you are NOT commissioned or delegated to be at this meeting; you BELONG here!

The word we have traditionally used for Ruling Elders at presbytery and everyone at Synod and GA is "commissioner". Commissioners are commissioned. I honestly don't know if in this electronic age it still happens, but a presbytery used to give a commissioner a piece of paper that was his/her commission and that commission had to be presented to a credentialing agent in order to be seated at the General Assembly (at least) as a commissioner. Of course, the work of the council is not hampered in the slightest little bit if people name their title incorrectly. But, words do matter and once we begin using them any old which way we rapidly lose track of why we used them in the first place.

In 1993 the grand proposal initiated by the UPCUSA Stated Clerk, Eugene Carson Blake and Episcopal Bishop James Pike in 1960, a proposal to unite the denominations of America into one church was losing momentum but was not yet dead. The effort, which began with the name of Consultation on Church Union, later to be called Churches United in Christ, had proposals on the table for cooperative ecumenical action. The reality was that the Reformed denominations (Presbyterian and Reformed Church in America, primarily) clung to the office of Ruling Elder in a way that the other participants had difficulty comprehending. They could not incorporate it and we could not give it up. The special committee acknowledged that while we maintained our ecumenical commitments we had problems with the state of this particular ecumenical effort. Time has made this final concern of the special committee, for the most part, irrelevant.

Chapter Four: Scripture and Reformed Heritage

As a community of believers in the triune God, called out and called together through God's Holy Spirit, the church bears witness to the life, death, and resurrection of Jesus the Messiah for the world's salvation. God's will is that there will always be a witness to God's power and saving grace (Matthew 16:13-19, Acts 14:17). God called the church to be that witness. [Nature of the Church report, page 6, citing a reference from Karl Barth.]

Based in Scripture

The Nature of the Church report follows its observation of the current situation with an extended summary of the call to and working of the church as it has grown out of the Scripture and been shaped by the Church's reflection on Scripture over the ages. Central to the report's argument is the following:

The Word of God incarnate in Jesus of Nazareth and written in the Old Testament (the Hebrew Scriptures) and the New Testament are authoritative for our understanding of the nature of the church. The Presbyterian Form of Government is based on our interpretation of these Scriptures (Confession of 1967, 9.27-30; Directory for Worship , 2.2001).

As the project to revise the Form of Government progressed over a generation, this understanding, that the Word of God, incarnate in Jesus Christ, lies beneath all the decisions and practices we describe for ourselves and follow in matters of governance, has stayed at the center of the work. Reading the Foundations section of the Book of Order is to see this heritage spelled out. Christ calls the Church into being through the testimony we find in the Scriptures. God's working to sustain God's community of faith is testified throughout the entire Biblical narrative. The principles around which we gather and out of which we govern find their initial reference points in the Scriptures. The confessions we affirm (all of them, not just ones that may be personal favorites) have reflected Scriptural authority throughout our history. Our Constitution - Confessions and Order - are standards against which we measure belief and practice, but always subordinate standards to the Scriptures.

As debates and discussions carried forward on how we wanted to govern ourselves, many believed that a particular Biblical passage or concern had not been given sufficient weight. Those concerns needed to be balanced with the understanding that the Form of Government, while it rests upon theological understandings found in Scripture is not itself intended to be, or to be used as, a Biblical treatise or a fully explored theology. The Form of Government is a document of governance reflective of and rooted in the Scriptures.

Documents describing governance are, all and all, rather pragmatic documents. The Foundations section of the BOO is one place where we dabble a bit more in the theologically colored material. One particular instance is in F-2.02. Here we find a Latin phrase, which, like most Latin phrases in common use, serves as a kind of mantra for a multiplicity of purposes.

Ecclesia reformata, semper reformanda secundum verbum Dei, that is, "The church reformed, always to be reformed according to the Word of God" in the power of the Spirit.

The affirmation that our opinions and practices of the moment are not and never were the full, complete and eternal reflections of Divine Will has been and continues to be foundational to our understanding of who we are. Of course that is also what tempts us toward, and sustains us in, endless debate as to who we are and what we are to be about!

In its section on The Biblical Witness, the Nature of the Church report cited this core phrase. They wrote: "The church is not enslaved to tradition; it lives by the renewing power of the Holy Spirit." They went on to affirm that openness to the Holy Spirit is the biblical basis for this Reformation principle. Whereupon they cited the Latin phrase, but translated it as, *the church reformed, always to be reformed, by the Word of God and the power of the Holy Spirit.* [Innocuously stating in an endnote, "this is translation (sic) other than what is in the Book of Order, G-2.0200.]

The current text chose to use the more extensive quotation, however it can be expected that discussion over the most helpful, or most "correct" translation of the phrase continues to be active. The current text reflects what many believe to be a superior translation in making it clear that the church is acted upon by God's Spirit in the continuing reforming of God's church. The motto invites us to look in the mirror and see ourselves as always reforming. Indeed, a comment the FOG revision task force heard along the way was that the denomination revises its constitutional documents about every twenty years. Some made the comment as a mark of something positive, while others leveled it as a criticism with a tone of voice suggesting "Oh no, not again!"

Change is certainly all around us and each of us must wrestle with it whether we like it or not. If everyone, or everything, is changing, how do I explain those who do not or who do not acknowledge the inevitable? (If it is inevitable.) Here's a story reflective of my wonderment:

When I was growing up (and for most lifelong Presbyterians of my vintage) Sunday morning worship looked something like this: We would gather and there would be a prayer of invocation, likely concluding with the Lord's Prayer. We would sing a hymn. A psalm would be read responsively and a lesson (usually only one) from Scripture would be read. An anthem would be sung by the choir, perhaps there was a children's message, the pastor would deliver the "long prayer" (Adoration, Confession, Thanksgiving,

Supplication, Intercession). The offering would be received followed by the sermon which may or may not reference the Scripture that was read earlier. Somewhere in the middle there had been another hymn sung and when we sang a final hymn the benediction was offered and we were away.

I won't take up space here to describe the history of how this order (there were variants, of course) evolved, or why. I read the "Directory for the Worship of God" from the 1820's to the 1950's, and the document remained virtually unchanged. The (sort of) worship order I described was fully consistent with the guidance offered pastors and sessions over all those years. Until the 1960's when a re-formation landed in the Presbyterian house. An academic discovery of the pre-Reformation orders of worship, combined with the changes in the Roman Catholic Church after Vatican II (rendering Roman Catholics less scary to the average pew-sitter) came to the forefront. Thus was created a movement loosely known as the Protestant Liturgical Renewal. Suddenly we discovered the wisdom and flow of ancient practices discarded as "popish". Lectionary preaching was encouraged. Our denomination reflected and created The Worshipbook, which contained suggested orders for worship consistent with these "new" discoveries. The Directory for Worship section of our Constitution was altered to encourage these new behaviors.

In church terms, the way we worshiped changed "overnight". Throughout my ministry, and now as I travel about in retirement, it is normative to follow the outline suggested in the Directory. Never the less, "normative" and "suggested" are the operative words. Our Constitution has always granted sole authority to the pastor and session of each congregation to order worship as they will. Unlike our more liturgically bound sisters and brothers, nothing is prescribed for us. If anyone is concerned that the alleged "local option" of the current text will lead to the destruction of our wondrous connectionalism; they need only wonder at the central and cosmic manifestation of session autonomy described in the Directory for Worship!

We have experienced in my lifetime a kind of reformation. Observing that however leads to its own curiosity. How do we explain those who are not changed? The question came to me on a visit to a large congregation (I mean really large, for us). The worship order was unchanged from the days of my youth. Now, the session has every right for that to be the way they worship. The pastors in that congregation are several and have been several for generations. They have every right to encourage the session to maintain that order. But it causes me to wonder.

For about 50 years, our constitutional documents have suggested a different form. All the pastors who have served that congregation for two generations have studied, been examined on, taken oaths, vows, or, if you don't like those words, answered affirmatively the questions prescribed in the Constitution. They vowed to be guided by these constitutional documents. All the elders who have served, every worship committee that has met and asked the question, what do we do and why do we do it, has chosen to look at and ignore, or not look at, the constitutional documents and the literature of our denomination's best minds. What is the organizational/congregational culture that leads to reforming?

If I understood that I would have a better sense of the prospects that the goal in revising the Form of Government, the goal of opening possibilities for congregations and presbyteries to become more fully agents of God's mission in the world, will be successful. I do not understand that, thus I trust the Spirit of the Living God, to melt us, mold us, fill us, use us - use even the likes of us, to further God's re-formation of the Church.

Back to talking about Scripture

Still exploring the Biblical Witness as context for our governance, the Nature of the Church report cited several Biblical references to illumine how we talk about the church. Then it provided as a summation: "The giving of gifts by the Spirit for the upbuilding and empowering of the body called for a hierarchy of love rather than of office. (I Cor. 12:27-14:1)"

It is an exegetical matter whether the great "hymn to love" in chapter 13 is the apostle's best exposition of the way we name and use leaders within the community, I will leave tht to others. It is certain that speaking of a "hierarchy of love" provides a vision of who we are and how we act with, toward and for each other that is in strong contrast to the secular governing environment in which we live; and, quite frankly, in strong contrast to how we have done much of the governing of the church in recent decades.

What is important in this current context is that the report points, through the Biblical witness, to the unique and central role we describe of "elders" in the life of the early church, and by implication for our understanding of Ruling Elders. The report amplifies this in an endnote, as follows:

Harper's Bible Dictionary (San Francisco: Harper, 1985), The entry on "presbyter" and "presbytery" ...is particularly helpful (p. 820).

(Gk. presbyteros, "elder"; presbyterion, "council" or "assembly of elders") a group of (usually older) men appointed to oversee the life of a congregation. The early Christian office of elder doubtless originated from OT and Jewish models (see, e.g., Num.11:16-17, 24-25). In NT times, each Jewish community had its council of elders (note the Sanhedrin in Jerusalem and "the elders" at Qumran). Paul and Barnabas appointed elders "in every church" (Acts 14:23; cf. 20:17-38; 1 Pet. 5:1-4; James 5:14; Rev. 4:4) In some instances, elder and "bishop" were apparently equated (Titus 1:5-9). For reference to a council of elders (presbytery), see 1 Tim. 4:14....

Out of this understanding, the Form of Government also restores to our use the title "Council" to describe the coming together of elders (Ruling and Teaching) to oversee, to decide, to lead, to guide, but especially to love the church. Over the past 50 years Presbyterians, in study after study, have broadened and diluted the definitions of the offices historically charged with leadership. I have no interest in challenging the notion that each and every believer, in baptism, is marked to fulfill the call and mission of Jesus. However, one great challenge before us is to recover distinct marks of those who are called and set apart for particular forms and functions of ministry within the community. Our practice defines three forms and functions to be Deacons, Ruling, and Teaching Elders. Perhaps it would be helpful to begin to describe these ordered ministries, and especially those designated as "elders" to be set apart for the primary purpose of loving the church.

An aside on Deacons

Here is how the Nature and Practice Report speaks of them. The office of deacon (Acts 6:1-6) met a crisis for service and leadership. It eventually become one of the established forms of ministry. How it came into being is instructive for the biblical pattern of leadership: the need arose, the apostles proposed a solution to the whole community; the qualifications were that those chosen would be Spirit-gifted and wise.

Acknowledging that the growth of the church led to a more complex pattern of service and leadership (some apostles, some teachers, some speakers-in-tongues, etc), the report suggests that cultural diversity and theological pluralism within the early church were addressed by councils; the councils of elders that we claim as the foundation of our system. The report acknowledges that in the contemporary church our concern to reflect our diversity and pluralism give us mandates that are not directly addressed by the practices of the early church. It asserts, however, that councils, met to resolve conflict, guided by the Holy Spirit, and that is the pattern we follow.

The report makes no attempt to alter the foundational definition of what persons are chosen as leaders. Those chosen are to be those who have demonstrated within the life of the community that they are "Spirit-gifted and wise". Or, as we find it in the FOG: "To those called to exercise special functions in the church ... God gives suitable gifts for their various duties. In addition to possessing the necessary gifts and abilities, natural and acquired, those who undertake particular ministries should be person of strong faith, dedicated discipleship, and love of Jesus Christ as Savior and Lord. Their manner of life should be a demonstration of the Christian gospel in the church and in the world." (G-2.0104a)

I look back over almost 50 years since I first felt that God was calling me to a particular ministry. I recall the days when I sought the concurring judgment of the Church in that call. It was a serious process. Then I think of any number of congregational nominating committees I have worked with over the years. I recall suggestions that we invite a certain person to serve as elder because "if he's on session, maybe he will get more active in the church." I remember nominations based on family ties, perceived financial wealth, and a dire need to get someone, anyone, willing to serve. Yes, 'tis true, God's Spirit can take any lump of clay and shape it into a sacred vessel. But if that is how we expect leadership to be shaped, we might just as well pull names out of a hat.

Our foundational understanding is that those chosen from among the community are to have already demonstrated that they are Spirit-filled and wise. Among the greatest struggles we have within our polity is the temptation to assert or quietly advocate that certain categories or groups of persons have a "right" to be represented in office. At the local level this can take the form of choosing the local CPA because we need someone for the Finance Committee or the schoolteacher who joined the church last month by adult baptism who would be a good addition to the Christian Education Team. But the struggle becomes even more difficult when we seek to develop a list of "protected categories" [Over the years the evolution of a list is present in F-1.0403 along with the implication that a certain "right" to participation attaches to membership in an enumerated group.] Despite the existence of such lists, when we seek to fill slots solely reflective of our particular perception of diversity we abandon our Scriptural and foundational principles and act in hope that somehow God's Spirit will take care of itself.

I am not suggesting going back to the days when elders were all male, were elected for life. It created its own problems. But I am also not comfortable with the implied "Theology of Rights" that leads us to examine persons in foundational terms almost as an after-thought to the categories they can fill in our template of diversity.

Ordained for Life

There are a couple of foundational assertions I believe all Presbyterians would affirm. (1) Officers are ordained for life. Once set apart for service, the only way to get out of it is to lay aside the ordination or be removed from office through judicial process. (2) Ordination is "to function". That is, one is set apart to a particular task/role/responsibility. Put next to each other in this fashion it is easy to see the way in which these two foundational understandings can be seen as contradictory in common practice. What happens to #1 if there is a change in #2?

Historically, elders were elected and served for life. (I once served in a congregation where one of the predecessor pastors had served for 33 years. During that entire time only a very small number of individuals had served on the session, and the Clerk, who was not an elder in active service had remained the same for about 30 of those years!) This pattern posed no problems for #1 & #2. A person was called to the session by the congregation and functioned in leadership, with the pastor, for the rest of his (for so it was) days.

But then, in the late 19th century we amended our Constitutional practice to allow for a rotational system of classes within the session as a local option. By the middle of the last century such a rotational system was mandatory. So it is that #1 remains in effect, but the full functioning of Ruling Elders in loving the congregation and caring for the members has been altered. In the minds of most individuals the expectation of a function in the role of an elder ends with the end of the term.

[A sidebar note:] Teaching Elders in those ancient of days were only ordained to serve as pastor to a parish. It was not uncommon for a pastor to serve his entire ministry in one parish. Moving on to some denominationally governed service as "evangelist" or "missionary" happened, but only after years in the parish. (Yes, I know there were some rare exceptions. The dispute over ordaining Charles Finney as an evangelist – after all he was the Billy Graham of his day – caused a great disruption in the 1830's.) By the 1950's, however, a wide range of "professional" activities had come to be engaged in by men (and then women) who had been previously ordained.

What becomes of the relationship between #1 (ordained for life) and #2 (serving a function in the Church) under these conditions? The solution for these folk is the process known as "Validation". Even if the activity engaged in is not under the governance of the denomination, we can declare that it is "as good as", hence we "sort of" baptize a function beyond our direct oversight. #2 is now covered! The membership category of For those whose vocational activity, ie. their "work", cannot be validated we have the category of Member at Large. Curiously, however, this process of declaring that a person retains #1 without a #2 reflects in practice a medieval, pre-Reformation, understanding that ordination is possessed by the person and is unrelated to fulfilling any particular function within the purview of the Body of Christ.

That is how we choose to address the situation of Teaching Elders. But what happens to those Ruling Elders (and deacons) whose "term" has ended? How does their experience clarify or confuse the meaning of ordination?

Ruling Elders, in our current reality, could easily be confused about just what their "office" in the church is, and isn't. Part of the confusion might well begin in the very ceremony of ordination itself.

Well into the middle of the last century, when elders were set apart, the ceremony did not so much reflect a "hierarchy of love" as one of authority. The vows that were taken were not as extensive or as (perhaps) rigorous as those taken by "Gospel Ministers". But, the Moderator called forth the vows and when the newly elected had affirmed them the Moderator led in prayer. In the Presbyterian Church in the USA that was all that was required. There was no Constitutional requirement of it, although it was quite common for the Moderator and perhaps the session to "lay hands" on the elder(s)-elect during this prayer. Either way, at the close of the ceremony or the worship service, the session members were directed to extend the right hand of fellowship to the newly ordained, welcoming them to this ministry. In the United Presbyterian Church in North America and in the Presbyterian Church in the United States (at the time of Reunion) the laying on of hands by the session was specified. In the UPCUSA after the 1958 union, the laying on of hands by the session became normative.

What catches our attention however is that it was the Moderator and perhaps the session (as the session) who had the authority to ordain and who carried it out. Recall that in practice, well into the 1950's the perception of most sessions would have been of a small group of male persons who for less than a generation had been mandated to be constrained by designated terms and practice class rotation. Certainly, in accepted practice the perception of a majority of members and elders was likely to have been that the pastor, as Moderator, conveyed the authority of the church (if not of Christ) to the elders who ruled in the congregation.

[As mentioned earlier, as late as my own ordination in 1970 in the UPCUSA, the parallel structure of ordination ceremonies determined that only the minister members of the presbytery participated in the laying on of hands. No elders participated in this ceremony. I recall how honored my family was that in my home congregation at the service led by the ministers who had been named to the ordaining commission, my Ruling Elder father was granted the privilege of "presenting" me to the presbytery for ordination.]

The rites and rituals by which we have set people apart for service reflect an understanding that this is serious spiritual business. These are the Spirit-gifted and wise ones entrusted to oversee and love the congregation in fulfillment of God's mission in the world. Control of these ordered ministries is important. The authority of the Church, represented by the appropriate council of session or presbytery, is essential. We maintain a doctrine of the "three part call" (ie. the movement of the Spirit, the presence of gifts for service and the approbation of the church). We assume that bearing office is important and to be treated with appropriate *gravitas*.

It is easy to begin to see the complexities and conundrums we have created. As an office held for life it is not to be accepted as "for this moment only", by first allowing and then mandating rotation in the office of Ruling Elder (a move approved for good and sufficient reason) an unintended side-effect appeared. How do we maintain an awareness of the awesome responsibility and obligation that is undertaken by submitting oneself to the power of the church as a Ruling Elder? If this historic understanding is diminished how do we retain a sense of engagement when a person is not in "active service"? How many times have I heard folk who are Ruling Elders speak of themselves as "lay people"? How many comments have begun, "Well, I'm only an elder, but…." How many have said, "I used to be an elder, but I'm not on the session any more."

I don't believe there is any cause-effect relationship, but clearly there was a parallel evolution of the ways in which the mainline Protestant denominations adopted corporate management forms and orders into their lives during the last century and the view by Ruling Elders that they were just "serving a term on the Board of Directors. Pastors are now seen as "staff" who are "hired" to carry out program. Teaching Elders (in even some of the smallest congregations) are described and often identify themselves as "Head of Staff" and behave as if they were the CEO of a business enterprise. Board members determine policy, staff members carry it out. When the term of elected service is ended they move on to other things and, in their own minds, return to being "just another church member."

Now, after more than a half a century of this understanding our services of ordination have taken on a different character. It is now the practice in most places, when it is time for the prayer and laying on of hands, all those who have been ordained are invited to come forward and surround the newly elected. I suspect that proponents feel such participation is a means of countering disengagement and reminding Ruling Elders that they are still ordained. However, often the result of the invitation is that virtually everyone comes forward. Now the member in the pew, rather than looking a small group of Gifted and Wise leaders who bear the burden of God's call, the few who are not invited forward could easily feel ashamed that they, of all these, have not yet been chosen! How strange a turn is that?

How the Nature of the Church Report Connects to the Current FOG

_The report of the Special Committee on the Nature of the Church and the Practice of Governance called attention to the documents of our heritage from the earliest days on through the Reformation.

Protestant reformers, including those of the Reformed tradition, claimed continuity with the catholic heritage of the church. Their aim was not to recreate the one, holy, catholic, and apostolic church, but to reform it. They claimed to be in accord with the teaching of the primitive church and the catholic church, and were not uninfluenced by catholic ideas of church order, ministry, discipline, and the church's role in society. Reformers raised the same questions asked for centuries, but gave different answers. The appeal, however, was not to tradition, but to Scripture.

The reader will note that the historic marks of the church, first affirmed in the Nicene Creed, that is, "one, holy, catholic and apostolic" are foundational to our understanding of how it is God has called the church into being. (F-1.0302)

Thinking about this heritage of re-forming, not re-inventing, the church, leads me to a form of the ubiquitous airport warning, "Don't leave your baggage unattended!" As we articulate that which is foundational to our practice of governance and reflect those foundational understandings into the ways in which we agree to live together, we dare not ignore the "baggage" we have brought with us from BEFORE the Reformation. AND, as an American denomination, we must also hang on to the great transformation of reformed ideas and practice that was made necessary by translating communities of faith from the "old country" to the "new".

In America, practices that had evolved out of centuries of seeking a way to be church in the context of monarchical and papal authority suddenly were re-constructed from the bottom up. Authority that had been culturally assumed to be divinely granted was now granted "by the consent of the governed". A tension, between seeing the Church (capital "C") as a divinely authorized body while in the new world seeing it as yet another voluntary association shaped and formed by its members, runs throughout our struggles to craft a meaningful and functioning Form of Government. There is baggage to be carried!

How do we view and respond to the "status" of ordination? On the one hand we argue that it conveys no status at all. One is ordained to a particular function. If a council of the church does not validate the function, then the ordination should (logically) go away. But the cultural expectations and personal validation of those who have been called by God to ministry and set apart through ordination (especially for Teaching Elders, Ministers of Word and Sacrament) is much more medieval in reality.

Ordination in the pre-Reformation understanding placed an irremovable mark on the person ordained. As the words of institution changed the bread and wine into actual body and blood, so too did the words of ordination change the very human character of the person such that he (and now, or she) was somehow imbued with special powers that were his and his alone. An ancient sounding phrase that disappeared with the revision described the role of Teaching Elder – in part – in this fashion: "And as he or she dispenses the manifold grace of God and the ordinances instituted by Christ, he or she is termed steward of the mysteries of God." (former G-6.0202a). The new wording is somewhat more prosaic, but captures a bit of the former sense in the phrase that the Teaching Elder is to "interpret the mysteries of grace." (G-2.0501) Once a person has been set apart to such a function, the notion that such wisdom would disappear with a "job change" is hard to envision.

Parity and the relationship between offices

As we have these three ordered ministries that we set apart by ordination, and as the offices of Ruling and Teaching Elder are essential to governance, it is reasonable to ask how the two relate. Here again we bring a good bit of "baggage" to the discussion.

Living as I do in an agricultural area, I have a subscription to a "farm paper". It keeps me informed on the issues my neighbors wrestle with on a daily basis. Recently a story caught my eye. The reporter was surveying the "percent of parity" reflected in the market value of various crops and commodities. I remember in the years of my growing up that "percent of parity" was a key concept in the discussion of federal agricultural commodity pricing policy. I had not heard the term or seen it discussed in years.

If you are not familiar with it, the begins with the market value during an established period in the past and computes the changes in input costs and inflation to establish what the comparable market value is today. The actual current market price is then described as a percent of that full value - or 100% of parity. Like any statistic it only proves what it proves and really so much has changed that I cannot guess its relevance beyond curiosity. But it is still an established benchmark to be considered.

Which brings us back to the Nature of the Church study. In considering our Reformed heritage the committee stated: "Our belief in the priesthood of all believers has many ramifications: ... parity of members and clergy and clergy with each other,"

A few years ago I was invited to write a piece on "parity" for HORIZONS Magazine, the journal of the Presbyterian Women. I hope I'm not violating some copyright provision by reproducing at length a portion of a first draft that I submitted to them.

Our reforming ancestors took over a church structure that was entirely controlled by the clergy. One principle they agreed upon in their Reformed Church was that there would be no hierarchy of clergy. A foundational understanding comes to us from that determination. All ministers of Word and Sacrament are equal to each other in authority and responsibility. This is the historical meaning of parity as used by Presbyterians.

From the first, ministers maintained membership in a separate body, the presbytery, where care was taken to see to it that congregations were safeguarded from false doctrine and shoddy preaching. "Ruling" elders were invited to sit with the ministers as the governing body for a particular church. As presbyteries evolved, ruling elders served as representatives from the congregations, seated alongside the minister members. When a vote was taken, ministers and ruling elders each had a vote, but they voted as two different types of "members" in the presbytery. A presbytery was simply a geographical district and there was no Constitutional concern as to how many of either category of member were eligible to vote.

As the American church evolved, in most presbyteries there ended up being a reasonable balance of ministers and elder commissioners. However there was no concern for equality. Up until the 1950's, larger parishes (Yoked Fields) served by one pastor were entitled to only one elder commissioner, if there was any anxiety in the system, it was that the ruling elders not become a majority.

Two things changed after World War II. A greatly increased number of (what we now call) specialized ministries altered the traditional pattern in which ministers served almost exclusively as parish pastors. Suddenly it seemed that there were more ministers than there used to be. Anxiety at this apparent inequity was intensified by a growing sentiment for "participatory democracy". Soon the Constitution was amended to make minister and ruling elder participation in presbytery more equal in numbers. As this change came to be fully implemented the use of the term parity came to define this equality of numbers between offices in governance. In this new way "parity" still spoke of who had access to the vote and the power that accompanied it.

Within the ongoing life of presbyteries (more so than other councils) questions are often raised regarding the relative numbers of Teaching and Ruling Elders and also the representation of persons representing various groups identified on the lists of categories of persons to be reflective of our diversity. Including persons on the basis of factors other than seeking those who are "Spirit gifted and Wise" trouble me. Quota systems are extremely problematic and to my mind wrong. But, and this is an important "but", we have expanded the definition of parity before. By removing some rigid structures and criteria from the FOG it is hoped that each council will seek the most faithful and effective ways of building a community of loving leaders for the life of the Church.

This is what the Nature of the Church report says:

The church believes itself true to biblical witness when it adapts its offices to meet current needs. [There follows this quotation from the Book Of Confessions 9.40] "Different orders have served the *gospel, and none can claim exclusive validity ... Every church order must be open to such reformation as may be required to make it a more effective instrument of the mission of reconciliation"*

We understand that foundational to our practice is the principle of representative governance. Councils of the church act based on the Spirit-guided decisions of representatives gathered. Hence we are neither hierarchical nor congregational in our polity. But representative of whom?

The Teaching Elders are the inheritors of the priestly function, the bishop's agent to oversee the life of the congregation and guard access to the mysteries of God. Ruling Elders accept the responsibility of governance for the congregation by service on the session. They represent an image of the congregation; seeking the Will of The Holy for the congregation. When such Elders, Teaching and Ruling come together in the council of a presbytery (and higher) they bring the collected image of the whole Church, the Church that exists in historical reality back to Christ and in the contemporary reality of a gathered congregation of believers.

I won't claim that the above paragraph is sufficient, but it reflects my sense of what we mean by representative governance. Out of that understanding I also raise what is to me a wonderment. I've described above that up until the twentieth century it was common for Ruling Elders to be participants in presbytery in numbers related to the pastors and not to the congregations. We changed that notion to entitle each congregation to a commissioned Elder, and, in the case of large congregations more than one. I'm cool with that. The church is the gathered faithful.

In that same time frame, however, the function of those who were presbytery members as Minister of the Gospel (old title) was almost exclusively composed of those serving as pastors of congregations. The proliferation of specialized ministers and those retired has swelled the rolls of many presbyteries such that in many if not most presbyteries almost every congregation is directed to double the number of commissioners to attain the equality of numbers we have also now affirmed as essential to governance. Reflecting on this two questions come to mind:

1.   What do we believe about the offices of Ruling and Teaching Elder that leads us to believe they naturally are in some oppositional stance requiring a balance of power? What awful thing would happen if the balance was left un-redressed?

2.   What leads us to believe that all Teaching Elders are gifted for governance? What if in the determination of what the mission of God required only some Teaching Elders were involved in governance? What if a separate structure - *The Venerable Company of Priests (John Calvin)* - was re-created as a forum in which Teaching Elders dealt with matters uniquely of their concern? What if a session determined that its moderator was neither interested in or gifted in governance and commissioned a gifted Ruling Elder to attend presbytery in his or her place?

If the offices of ministry are indeed subject to constant RE-FORMATION, I find these to be interesting questions?

The American Experience and the Corporate Church

 Born of Reunion - as was the Nature of the Church report itself - Milton Coalter, John Mulder and Louis Weeks (all, at the time, associated with Louisville Theological Seminary) undertook the task of editing a multi-volume collection of essays on the place of Presbyterianism in the twentieth century. "The Presbyterian Presence" series sought to set a context around experience. In an abbreviated way so did the Nature of the Church report. One extended quotation from the "Presence" series that is included in the report catches the eye:

In the twentieth century the corporate denomination became the dominant image of the church for Presbyterians. The denomination as a corporation is a bureaucratic, hierarchical organization dependent on managers and capable of delivering goods and services to congregations as well as mobilizing and coordinating support of national and international mission causes. The characteristics of incorporation permeated national structures as well as congregations. [1]

At this point the special committee report commented that the church had "been uneasy with this corporate model" because of varying understandings of leadership and an alleged conflict between goals for evangelism vís a vís mission, and/or personal versus public ministries. I think they only got half the picture. The style of secular corporate management is contrary to the representational model of our tradition. That is true. However, it seems that the members of the special committee still accepted that the end product of denominational activity could be described as the "delivery of services" and that such was an appropriate goal. The last few decades have demonstrated that the fusion of ecclesiastical and programmatic work under one head and style has not worked. The style was inappropriate but also the program delivered did not engage the people in the pew sufficiently for success.

Why didn't it work? Well, one could argue (as some do) that the goals endorsed were contrary to Scripture. Or, it could be said that the leadership did an inadequate job of communicating, I've heard each one said and uttered some of those very words myself. It seems that a more significant claim is that it didn't work because it was fundamentally and foundationally in conflict with and contradiction of our polity. The idea that the mission of the church could be defined at the level of the General Assembly and then administratively and effectively passed down to the pews, as McDonalds might specify correct content and procedures for hamburgers or General Motors might direct the sale of Pontiacs to the driving public, was doomed from the start.

Such notions were doomed by an observation the Nature of the Church report had made clear but a page earlier. "(I)n the American church, the presbytery was the originating authority, relating particular churches into a larger whole. The 1788 Form of Government declared that ...*no act of a General Assembly could become a standing rule without first being referred to the presbyteries and securing the consent of at least a majority of them.*"

The argument was (and I suspect still is made by elected members and staff of the General Assembly Mission Council) that determinations in matters of "mission" are different from determinations in matters of "law". But that's a dichotomy flawed to its core. Experience has only confirmed what was suspected in 1992; the whole idea of a strong, centralized, national church has become ineffective in contemporary America. In addition it has virtually no foundational support in our heritage.

Many have commented with humorous irony that we are denomination held together by our polity. Interestingly enough, the movements of the corporate church in the 60's and 70's to restructure mission into centralized forms ignored the core polity assumptions that formed the foundation of the mission. In effect those efforts created a mission structure and practice in conflict with polity. Whether inadvertently or by design national practice was carried out as if polity were irrelevant in matters of mission. We now live in a denomination in which a generation of local leaders no longer feel that the central assumptions of polity are relevant to mission and thus to polity. Few feel any constraint upon any local activity. Thus we cling to a polity without understanding and law without gospel. Most who think of polity at all seek only the protections of a strong set of laws intended to permit and prohibit what their personal persuasions dictate.

[1] Coalter, et. al., The Re-Forming Tradition, Louisville, W/JK Press, 1992, pg 101

Chapter Five: Recommendations

The Nature of the Church and the Practice of Governance committee was initiated by the General Assembly in 1989. Their report was acted on in 1993. During the intervening years (if they behaved typically) they likely held two to four meetings a year, each one lasting a couple of days. (My experience is that guilt about spending the church's money leads such groups to hold marathon daily meetings lasting from 8 AM to 10 PM with minimal breaks for meals - volunteers work hard for the privilege of service!) Their report indicates an extensive bibliography of papers prepared specifically for their consideration by a range of scholars within the church, as well as a broad range of books and papers from other sources. This was a serious study by serious people!

The report concluded with a series of recommendations for action. And, as is most often the case when big concerns yield multiple recommendations, almost none of them were approved by the Assembly to which they were presented! Because recommendations that are not enacted tend to disappear from view, the printed document currently available to the church at large is the result of the General Assembly's action in receiving the report. The recommendations are not included. The Minutes of the General Assembly for 1993, 26.205ff are where they may be located. They were:

Section A – Governing Bodies

Recommendations #1-4 address a desire to differentiate clearly between *ecclesiastical* and *programmatic* work.

As noted above, prior to the reorganizations of the late '60s, judicatories/governing bodies/courts of the church had been primarily (to the point of exclusively) concerned with ecclesiastical business. The programmatic activities, the support of educational tasks, and other tasks within the denomination and the service and witness to the world beyond the church, were in the hands of semi-independent boards and agencies that the General Assembly authorized and reviewed but did not directly control. [There were perceptual variations between northern and southern streams, but in essence they were similar.] After reorganization all the activities were combined within the structure of the General Assembly itself and at the level of synods and presbyteries. "Mission" appropriate to the setting was to be designed and implemented after vertically oriented negotiation. Where in the past, lines had been clear, now the boundaries between agents of action and agents of oversight were blurred. Often both functions were vested in the same person(s).

The initial section of the report made four recommendations: First, that the "unity" of the church be refined to specify that it was in its ecclesiastical activity that we found our unity, not in our programmatic work. As the report framed it "The church finds its unity in its ecclesiastical nature, and welcomes diversity and richness of expression in its mission and program" The language of G-9.0103 specifies that governing bodies are separate and independent but act in such mutuality that the act of one is the act of all. The primary historic impact of implied unity had to do with the ordination of ministers. A mission program or advocacy activity that may be right and proper in one region may not be seen as such in another locale. Hence, to avoid potential conflict and misunderstanding, the report sought to insert "ecclesiastical" before the word "act" in this paragraph. This proposed change was sent to the presbyteries and it was defeated.

The second proposal also addressed (then) G-9.0103. To reinforce that we could have unity without mandating programmatic uniformity, a phrase was to be added to the end of the paragraph specifying that powers not mentioned in the Constitution are "reserved to the presbyteries". Given that presbyteries, in so far as they ordain ministers and organize congregations, are central to the very existence of the denomination and must approve any Constitutional changes, this is a reasonable assertion. The presbyteries apparently found it to be so, and this amendment was approved and stands in the Constitution today.

Interestingly, this had not been the longstanding position of the church and as late as the 1958 union of the PCUSA and the UPNA the exact opposite position was taken, that the General Assembly possess authority for anything unmentioned. Thus, decisions on mission at the session and presbytery level are constrained by the language of the Constitution. If not specifically permitted, then it is forbidden. The balance of argument tips between unity on the one hand and authority on the other. With this 1993 amendment the scale tipped to the side of presbytery authority against denominational unity, although practical politics could argue this only stated the obvious. While I have never heard the point made, this shift could have motivated an intensification of the move to specifically bar the ordination of "avowed and practicing" homosexuals as presbytery autonomy was now strengthened.

In part I think the shift was felt to be required because shifting the responsibility and authority for "mission" to the synods, presbyteries and sessions required it. However, one phrase was left out of the recommendation as it was proposed to the presbyteries. The report requested the amendment read ...reserved to the presbyteries, *which may delegate those powers to other governing bodies or units under G-9.0403,* and with the acts...." One stated goal of reorganization was to decentralize mission and assign responsibility to the governing body most closely connected to the work to be done. This required that unity be sacrificed to service and that authority and control be distributed. The reorganization assumed that much of the mission determination would be vested in presbyteries and synods. Work is to be assigned to those most equipped or available to carry it out. The

phrase about delegation was not approved by the General As[sembly]
on to the presbyteries for a vote. Why? It likely was seen as re[...]

The third recommendation in this section addressed the mor[...]
authorized to decide?" It had always been clear that the eccle[...]
church had been in the hands of those who bore office. Ministers and Elders composed
the courts of the church and only they could vote. Now, with programmatic activity
included in the decision making, circumstances came up whereby persons vital to the
program of the church may not also be office bearers. To preserve the historic role of
ordained offices in authority, the report recommended "*Participation in governing body actions
is limited to ministers of the word and sacrament and elders.*" Those who were neither could be
granted corresponding member status, could be allowed to speak, but could not vote in
any body, or any body to which the work of the governing body may be delegated. In the
populist spirit of the time and the ever-growing consensus that baptism, not ordination,
was the primary qualification for service, this recommendation was not approved or
submitted to the presbyteries for a vote.

The fourth and final recommendation in this section sought to clarify the individual roles
of persons, seeking to keep some clarity of understanding between the ecclesiastical and
the programmatic. A series of clarifying statements were proposed to delineate the roles
of Moderators, Clerks and Administrative Staff. Governing bodies were urged to "honor
the distinction between governance and administration". Specifically, an appeal was made
to governing bodies not to combine the role of Executive and Clerk in the same person.

The report's rationale can be summarized in this statement, "*The distinction between that
which is ecclesiastical and that which is programmatic is very important in Presbyterianism. It is the
difference between policy-making and decision-making on the one hand, and implementation and
resourcing on the other; between officers and staff; between authority and service. Governance belongs to the
governing body. Governance is maintenance of the body, preparing for mission. Mission is the
implementation by the body of the mission determined through its decision-making function, the
governance. Councils and administrative staff remain subject and accountable to the decision-making and
policy-making power of governing bodies.*"

None of these recommendations were approved and sent down for consideration. The
fusion and confusion between governance and program continued. Executive or General
Presbyters combined with the office Stated Clerk (and sometimes Treasurer) proliferated.
Presbytery Councils labored mightily to make meetings "interesting" by moving more and
more of the ecclesiastical (read boring) business to the margins or by delegating full
authority to sub-units. Amendments to the Constitution allowing "members" to serve in
various capacities - as opposed to ministers or elders exclusively - continue to be brought
forward and many were approved.

commendation # 5

Every special committee, every standing committee, every human community charged
with a task, likely ends up picking up stray threads here and there and seeks to knit them
into the fabric work. All in all, over the years, I marvel at the power of the Holy Spirit to
take a group of faithful Presbyterians, give them a task fraught with difficulties and
potential pitfalls, and lead them to a wise and right decision. So, I cannot complain when
I am taken by surprise.

In this case, recommendation number 5 of the committee report seems to come from
nowhere. It is concerned for the authority to authorize the celebration of the Lord's
Supper. Governing Bodies (G-9.0102b) have/had authority to authorize the Sacrament.
But what happens when there is not time to take the action? When the proposed
amendment was sent down to the presbyteries (where it was approved and now stands as
a part of W-3.6204(1)) the rationale for approval said it would provide "flexibility" and
implied a context of General Assembly or Synod special events or gatherings at which the
Sacrament was desired but the planning of which did not allow a formal authorization by
the sponsoring governing body. So, since presbyteries meet more frequently, the
amendment would permit the presbytery in which an event is to be held to authorize the
Sacrament.

The full recommendation first "urges" governing bodies that meet infrequently to
establish policies that define just what types of sub-groups and what sorts of events
qualify as settings in which the Sacrament would indeed be authorized. Presumably a
presbytery asked to approve such an event could refer to these criteria to determine if the
authorization was appropriate. [1]

But what are the issues? What are the dangers? Why did the matter come to be in the
report? There is nothing in the way of clues in the body of the report itself. I see two
possible concerns.

First, the special committee clearly was concerned about the role and functions of
"officers" in the life of the church. In the argument about what powers and authority is
to be restricted only to Teaching and Ruling Elders versus that which can be shared with
church members the tension is evident. The stream of understanding that asserts a
primacy of baptism over ordination is not so subtly at work here. The committee leaned
toward drawing authority more closely into the circle of those who were ordained. On
the other hand, the Advisory Committee on the Constitution, in its advice on the report
is opposed to restricting programmatic leadership to ordained officers only, although they
did not oppose this amendment.

Second, I believe the committee saw this as an extension of its concern with the impact
of the "corporate" style of the church as opposed to its "spiritual" reality (again, debates

well argued in the mid-nineteenth century). That governing bodies were too focused on program at the expense of well-ordered worship led them to a concern for the stewardship of the mysteries of God and a residual desire to in some way "guard the table" against a kind of *loosey-goosey* notion that any group could self-authorize the Sacrament and observe it at any time and place.

Section B, - Representation

The next section of recommendations in the report encourages "encouragement". Governing Bodies are encouraged to examine the way folk are elected to more inclusive governing bodies to insure that those persons are "gifted by the Holy Spirit to discern the will of God through governance." And, it encourages the reporting back from those commissioners to be more seriously considered. It urged minister members not serving as parish pastors to be involved in the life of the presbytery or a congregation. What could prompt such seemingly self-evident encouragement? Our foundational understanding is that governance is carried out in representative bodies of balanced numbers of ruling and teaching elders who deliberate (carefully and prayerfully) seeking to discern what the Will of God is for the Church. In this deliberation and discernment they are not to be guided by the popular will or directed by constituencies, stake-holders, or interest groups, but by the Spirit of God as best that Spirit's intent can be determined.

The Constitution is clear that once members and commissioners come together at a meeting their ONLY guide is to be the movement of the Holy Spirit; while the committee dared not come right out and say it, they also felt an inherent tendency in the way we had come to do our business that the process of choosing commissioners and how those folk saw themselves was unduly influenced by factors contrary to this principle. Further, it seemed clear that the relationship between councils (to use the current term) was hampered by a lack of shared knowledge and interaction. The often perfunctory reporting from the commissioners did a disservice to the expectation that decisions would be shared and affirmed by all.

This lack of engagement is exemplified by the actions of those Teaching Elders who are virtually absent, absent from the deliberations of the presbytery that issues their credentials and claims them as members. If the members do not treat the body seriously and the commissioners come without knowledge or with prejudice, how is the Spirit expected to do her work?

That we have come (often) to treat our deliberative assemblies so cavalierly, and as if they were secular political entities, subject to the pull and tug of competing ideologies and claims, opens us to the challenge; just who is being served?

And that leads me to the word that dare not be spoken.

In the midst of a Committee on Ministry meeting some time back, the topic under consideration led me to one of those "old guy" observations that "in the olden days" our ordination vows (and they were still thought of as vows and not just answers to questions) bound us to "subjection to (our) brethren in the Lord". Upon hearing that word, subjection, a more newly ordained minister blurted out, "If that had been the question when I was ordained, I don't think anyone in my whole class at Princeton would have been ordained!" Subjection to a presbytery, to the body, is not on the radar screen. In too many instances Teaching Elders see themselves as self-motivated, self-authorized, degree-certified individuals with a Presbyterian "union card". Ordained for the good of the whole denomination is made subject to their reception of God's Spirit and answerable only to the reasonableness of whatever spiritual discipline they find works for them.

In those same "olden days", the service of installation asked the congregation: "Do you promise to receive the word of truth from his(sic) mouth with meekness and love and to submit to him(sic) in the due exercise of discipline?"

How strange it sounds to our ear that in accepting God's call and seeking the approbation of the church in pursuing and then receiving a call to ministry we should vow that we put ourselves in a position of subjection to our brethren. And, who are we that we should even consider for a minute that those who sit in the pew before us should in any way meekly and lovingly pay attention to what we say and change their behavior when we suggest that the Lord might require it?

Before we celebrate that the priesthood of all believers reflective of our common ministry in baptism has, God be praised, removed such medieval notions as subjection and submission from our understanding and practice; let's not dismiss too quickly that the Church is a different kind of organization. Our connections and relationships are organic, such that the hand cannot think of saying to the arm or the eye, "I have no need of you". In that no part of the whole can exist without full engagement with every other part, the notion that we are, all, each, and every, subject to, submissive before, and entirely dependent on all each and every other part of the whole is a foundational notion. At core, the special committee was seeking to reassert that minister members and commissioners came together as equals but also as those beholden only to God's Spirit and to each other.

The intersection of this organic unity and the principles of governance is captured in the Foundational section at F-3.0202. *This church shall be governed by presbyters, that is, ruling and teaching elders. Ruling elders are so named not because they "lord it over" the congregation (Matt. 20:25) but because they are chosen by the congregation to discern and measure its fidelity to the Word of God, and to strengthen and nurture its faith and life. Teaching elders shall be committed in all their work to equipping the people of God for their ministry and witness.*

The nature of the Church, as we understand it, and the practice of governance as we seek to affirm it, rely not on power, or competitive advantage, or seeing to it that our understanding is the only understanding. No, the nature of the church and the practice of governance relies on mutual subjection whereby my skills, my training, my opinion, my advantage are always submitted to our skill, our training, our opinion and our advantage as we determine it by discerning the Will of God for the Church by the Holy Spirit.

Subjection is a tough word, but it's a word we need to speak and seek to recover in our working vocabulary.

There was one substantive recommendation in the committee's section on representation. This had to do with large membership congregations. I have written above of the evolution in the twentieth century toward a numerical equality between the minister members and elder commissioners and of the effect specialized ministers and retired ministers had on this discussion. Now, we come to a recommendation of the Nature of the Church report that addresses another aspect of the issue.

The ruling elders who comprise the "commissioners to presbytery" side of the equation are, of course, all to be "Spirit guided and wise" for such is the nature of the office. But in the spirit of a kind of "populist" democracy and the outflow of the secular emphasis on "one man (sic) one vote", it was deemed (in the 1983 Reunion Constitution) to be un-representative for a 500-member congregation with two ministers and a 2000+ member congregations with two ministers to have the same number of commissioners. The larger the congregation, (in increments of 500) the more commissioners it should be assigned. However, that increase was capped at 2000. The recommendation was that above 2000 members the formula be changed to assign an added commissioner for each additional 1000 members.

The impact this change had on actual practice is, of course, minimal. There are enough extra ministers on the roll (in virtually all presbyteries) to allow assigning a few extra commissioners. The number of congregations over 2000 is still minuscule and only the largest presbyteries are likely to have one, let alone more. This was an easy "fix" to a problem no one cared much about (save a few in very large congregations who got exercised by the per capita assessment and wanted to use their supposed 'lack of representation' as an arguing point to hyperventilate on other issues.

But raising it does bring up again just what we mean by representation. I have dealt with it from several points of view. As a Stated Clerk it was my task to worry about proposing a way to balance the representative equation. As an Executive Presbyter it was my task to interpret both the responsibility of ruling elders in the higher governing bodies and the meaning and function of those governing bodies when seeking to explain per capita assessments to those who did not like paying them. Most importantly, as a pastor of a larger congregation it was my job to try and convince numbers of ruling elders to actually participate as commissioners. This, and perhaps in all three tasks, I confess to having often been a miserable failure.

Meetings of presbytery over the last 16 years of my parish ministry were routinely at least a ninety minute to a two hour drive away. Participation consumed an entire day or drive late into the evening. In other words, it took greater dedication than I was able to engender or a greater sense of guilt than I was capable of inflicting, to encourage ruling elders to attend. The business of the meeting seemed often disorganized, arcane, and/or irrelevant to the uninitiated. Indeed, even minister members were often disengaged or disdainful of the work. Meeting planners worked hard to make meetings educational, or entertaining, but educating the disinterested and entertaining the guilt-ridden is no easy task!

The goal was consistency and sessions were urged to appoint commissioners for terms of up to three years. But the formula for allocating extra commissioners rewarded those who actually sent them and "punished" those who were able to fulfill their quota at less than a 50% rate. Hence, one year our session would be assigned 5 commissioners, which we were never able to fill, so that the next year we would be assigned our usual two commissioners, which we always managed with ease. This seesaw effect did nothing to enhance any sense of gravity in the process.

I have no simple answers to this awkward matter of how we go about moving our foundational understanding of representative governance into the practical world of real life. For the time being, presbyteries will simply need to wrestle in any way they are able to compose themselves of commissioners who are Spirit-guided and wise. The FOG seeks to offer some flexibility and I suspect the Spirit will be able to figure something out

There was another recommendation in this section of the report: *"that the 205th General Assembly (1993) urge sessions, pastors, and specialized ministers to explore the parish associate or other active role in the life a particular church or presbytery."*

The background rationale in the report itself is not of much help in assessing what gain the committee hoped would come from this urging, save that every minister member of presbytery would be active in either a presbytery and/or a particular congregation. But what assumptions can we make from the need for urging involvement? Only the assumption that some are not so active?

Yes, that is most likely the case. The demarcation of "Parish Associate" came into both streams of the tradition in the 1970s. I cannot speak to the PCUS action, but the rationale at the time the provision was inserted in the UPCUSA Constitution was clear. The reality was that many specialized minister members of presbytery had no regular participation in any worshiping congregation of this denomination. The activism of the time and the antagonism of many against "the establishment" aggravated this reality with evidence of non-participation being amplified by outright disdain for the very structures that gave Teaching Elders their credentials. The thought was that, perhaps if we gave persons a "title" they would be more likely to become involved.

That the provision was hedged round with a considerable number of requirements indicates something of the trepidation with which it was approached. The specifics were and are rather elaborate for the nature of the position. A pastor invites another member of presbytery to be a part of the life of the congregation by granting a title. The session approves the pastor's invitation, the presbytery grants the designation and once a year the granted title is reviewed. If the pastor leaves, the title goes away.

Perhaps it achieved its desired objective. Perhaps ministers content to read the Sunday newspaper and watch Robert Schuller or "Meet the Press", were now, in hopes of a title worthy of their calling, attracted into the pews. I never saw that happen. Those already involved in the life a congregation stayed involved and some were given a title.

But the unintended consequences were widespread. Soon the flexibility about there being specific tasks and/or compensation came to be a framework in which actual pastoral work came into the hands (along with a second income) of those with the title. In an earlier time there had been the designation of "Assistant Pastor". The UPCUSA Constitution phrased it: *An assistant pastor is a minister nominated by the pastor and invited by the pastor and session to assist the pastor in any department of his work. The relation shall be established between the assistant pastor, the session, and the presbytery. Any change in this relationship must be approved by the presbytery. No formal call shall be issued by the congregation. ... It is understood that the agreement between the session and an assistant pastor may, whenever a pulpit becomes vacant, be terminated upon due notice.....* [UPCUSA Form of Government, Chap. XX, 1, 1965-66] Sound familiar?

In recent times, Parish Associates may serve simply as window dressing. In many instances Parish Associates serve as *de facto* assistant pastors. Problems easily arise when congregation members, without understanding our theology of called ministry, become upset with the requirement that their much beloved Parish Associate may not continue in service when the pastor leaves.

While the stated reason for creating the title was, as I said above, to encourage involvement in congregations by specialized ministers, the shape and outcome suggest a more complex possibility. The foundational principle involved is that in the congregation the right of the people to elect those who serve in positions of leadership/authority among them is inalienable. That was part of the rationale for doing away with the Assistant Minister title since the congregation had no hand in their selection or retention. The politics at the time was heavily influenced by the argument that pastors in picking their colleagues would discriminate against women ministers. At a time when more and more women were seeking ordained positions, finding opportunities for called service was critical. The logic was that the Constitutional mandates on the search process and the broader influence of elected committees would more likely give women a fair chance.

The strange twist of history was that this change was made right at the time that more and more pastors in position to influence the calling of a second ordained person came to value the diversity that women could bring to the staff team. The Assistant Minister protocol allowed women to be chosen and brought into leadership by the will of a pastor. With its elimination it was discovered that congregationally elected committees tended to be much more traditional in their outlook, fearing their congregation "not yet ready for a woman". The result was that a change seeking to be helpful became a barrier.

The use of the Parish Associate relationship is now within the purview of each presbytery. Does it continue to have a meaningful place? Only time and practice will tell.

Section C - Inclusivity

The next recommendation in the report deals with diversity and the inclusion of diverse folk within the community. Dealing with diversity as a matter of institutional formation has been, for the past 40 years or so, the sticky wicket above all sticky wickets for the Presbyterian community. The predominant theological and ethical ethos among our leadership has long affirmed the vision of a community welcoming and inclusive.

However, the issue before the Nature of the Church study and report was not primarily theological or ethical. The concern was "How and to what extent do we place organized ethical behavior into constitutionally mandated practice?" To what extent are we able to trust that, given theological and ethical mandates, governing bodies of the church will do the right thing? Or, on the other side, if governing bodies fail to do the right thing, what mechanism to we put in place to correct them?

At the time of reunion a complicated formula was put in place. Structurally it sought to control the outcome of processes, processes designed to reflect foundational understandings of authority and responsibility.

In other words, while presbyteries were seats of original jurisdiction and free to organize themselves within certain boundaries - that is each must have certain mandated ecclesiastical committees - the freedom to form those committees was further constrained by certain categories. Further, a special committee must be formed to "hold the body's feet to the fire" in order to "guarantee" conformity to the theological and ethical standards of inclusiveness. This special committee was designated the Committee on Representation and it was to be composed of at least five persons. One each from, the majority male, majority female, minority male, minority female and youth populations of the body. This group would be responsible to consult, advocate, and advise the governing body and especially its nominating committees and staff selection processes. Reports were to be filed annually with higher governing bodies.

This Committee on Representation continues in the Constitution (G-3.0103) along with a statement that the functions of this committee can not be merged with any other entity or committee.

I suppose the principle question that can be asked of any mandated structure or practice is: Does it function and does it achieve its objectives? My own observation would be that the answers are "No" and "Yes". The governing structures and practices of councils reflect our diversity to an extent unimaginable a generation or two ago. Has some kind of perfect reflection of the diversity within the body been achieved? Probably not. But nominating committees have sought out persons reflective of the "protected categories" defined by the Constitution and urged them to accept service within the governing body. Our leaders firmly believe in the theological and ethical mandate of an inclusive church. We ought not be proud and should never be satisfied, but we need not apologize for the way in which we have sought to present ourselves to each other and to the world.

The reality of a Committee on Representation has been more complex. What we create is a committee whose purpose is not to produce work in/of the body but to monitor the way the body does its work. This is a committee charged to advocate for certain categories of persons, in essence a political strategy that seeks principally to move and shape the decisions and actions others are charged to fulfill. This committee advises behaviors without having directly to live with the consequences of that advice.

For instance, a person recruited to fill a slot on a committee in which they have little interest, working in a structure for which they may possess few gifts is not likely to be particularly productive member. In a large number, if not most presbyteries, the reality of the committee has hardly, if ever, lived up to expectations. I won't say that this "failure to thrive" is good, bad, or indifferent. It is, for me, an observable reality that it hasn't worked very well.

I don't believe my observation is new. The limitations on this piece of mandated structure were already obvious and the 1993 report recognized it and sought to amend the Constitution to merge the function into the work of the Nominating Committee itself. That was defeated in the presbyteries and led to the mandated provision that indeed the functions could not be combined. The drafting task force sought to give presbyteries flexibility in all structures, but the forces seeking to maintain this structure were mightier. There is to be a committee and presbyteries are not free to seek to improve their behavior outside such a committee's work, even if the established practice is ineffective.

s around our diversity is still of great importance in the life of the ͜ᴗ.ᴜnation. Nevertheless, regulatory mandates have been largely removed. For better or worse, the FOG allows each council of the church to determine for itself how best to reflect the theological and ethical call to affirm diversity into its institutional life. We say that the community cannot exist save by "trust and love". That's not entirely true. We do also have administrative review. The mandate still stands. We welcome all and include all. We are challenged to make administrative review a bit more rigorous than simply verifying that the proper committee has been formed in order to determine that a council has fulfilled the mandate.

Section D - Session and Congregation

The next section of recommendations in the Nature of the Church report is headed "Session and the Congregation". Their introduction reminds us of two aspects of the special committee's mandate: "The growing use of decision-making styles and procedures which reflect organizational theories which may not reflect Presbyterian principles of governance" and "[t]he presence of distinct experiences and practice of governance emerging from the different racial and ethnic communities within our Presbyterian Church (U.S.A.)" [Minutes, 1989, Part I, p. 121]

The committee asked the General Assembly to affirm that: (a) sessions are unique and vitally essential to governance; (b) sessions are deliberative bodies responsible for mission and governance of the particular church; (c) Pastors and elders are responsible for SHARED leadership (my emphasis); (d) sessions must train elders and congregations in Presbyterian governance; and (e) sessions are to encourage participation by elders and members alike in higher governing bodies as a reflection of the inter-related nature of our denomination.

These recommendations challenge two widely distributed failings in current practice. In no order of priority they are: (1) that we allow ruling elders to view their role as "serving a term on the board of directors", and (2) that when they are serving, many are inadequately trained to be ordained in our foundational understandings of the office of Ruling Elder.

Actually, there is an order of priority there. Because of the shift to mandating rotation of persons in and out of defined terms of office, the tendency to see the place of the ruling elder as a "board member" came to be built into the system. A board member is somewhat removed from the day-to-day operation of most organizations. A board member, in a charitable organization may have a niche that he or she fills and may even be wholly responsible for some aspect of the program. But that is not as a member of the board. Rather, in most cases the person is on the board because they fill a niche. The board becomes then, at the very least, a collection of stakeholders. In larger, more complex organizations, those with hired employees, particularly "professional" hired employees, the proper role of the board member is to oversee the work that the staff carries out toward fulfilling the organization's objectives. Indeed, good training of board members encourages this distinction between policy and practice. More than once in my life, serving on various boards, I have lamented time spent in board meetings reviewing the long distance phone bill or charges for postage stamps purchased, rather than wrestling with the "big picture" issues appropriate to a board.

Is it at all possible that we might free ourselves from this phenomenon while maintaining the mandate for rotation and terms? Personally, I doubt it, but such a radical shift is not a part of the current discussion. There are likely creative alternatives to move away from current practice. Surely, however, no change will occur unless we are able, through training and education, to completely recast the understanding of teaching and ruling elders and the congregations that elect them.

I know there are sessions that take their educational role seriously and carry out elaborate and extensive curricula for fulfilling the mandate to train and approve those whom the congregation elects. Most (I suspect this to be true, for it was certainly my practice.) are grateful if they can get the newly elected in the same place as the current session for a period measured in hours in an effort to minimally inform and motivate an understanding that serving as an ordained officer in the church is different than being "a member of the board." We pray for this educational experience to have the desired effect.

Presbyterians believe in education. We demonstrate at every governing body level and virtually in every meeting our belief that if people only have the correct information they will do the right thing. We are so convinced of this that we throw the same Biblical passages, the same author's articles, the same rational arguments at our audience time after time, as if mere repetition of the arguments we consider righteous will eventually break through opposition that is seen simply as ignorance. You shall know the Truth (unfortunately, we mean OUR Truth) and that truth will transform the person.

As you might gather from the above, I doubt it will happen. Under our Constitution, governance relies on ruling elders, and teaching elders coming together and collectively functioning as Spirit-guided and wise rulers. This collaboration requires the whole person, not just the reasoned person to be fully engaged. For these wise rulers to have an awareness of who and whose they are that goes beyond being once a month board members will require more than education, it will take Holy Spirit instilled transformation.

If I haven't already implied it with sufficient clarity, I will say it straight out. The system of mandatory terms and rotation for those called by God to serve in the office of Ruling Elder in the church has deprecated, diminished and (permanently?) destroyed the office as it stands in our foundational and historical understanding.

That is not to say that there are not individual elders who are deeply Spirit-guided and wise. I cannot count the numbers of faithful women and men who have taken term after term over their lives, each and always seeking to follow the One who called them to this ministry. It is the now almost century old mandate that the office is something that is put on and taken off from time to time that has minimized its stature in the Church. Yes, I know we say that the office is perpetual and that those not in active service are still Ruling Elders. But we do little or nothing to enact that assertion in the life of our congregations. There was/is something to be said (at least metaphorically) for the days when elders were elected for life and sat on a bench beneath the pulpit facing the congregation as the community gathered each Lord's Day.

This little bit of diatribe is motivated by the final recommendations of the Nature of the Church report as it has to do with sessions and congregations. The topic before them had to do with congregations requesting exemption from the requirements of rotation and the required composition of the nominating committee. The report acknowledges that certain congregations need the allowance of flexibility (therefore a good idea) and also that the requirement that presbytery hears the reasons and grants the exception seeks to maintain order.

However, this strange sentence sits in the middle of the committee's argument: *"Serving on the session or the board of deacons affords a greater opportunity to be strengthened by the study of Scripture, the Constitution, and prayer."* Doesn't this sound like the presentation so often heard in congregational nominating committees that "Let's ask Jim to be an elder, I'm sure he'd start attending worship if he were on session." It is the obligation of the session to provide for the congregation ample opportunities for the study of Scripture and polity. Prayer is the lifeblood of all we do. But service on session is not where a person of faith acquires the benefits of such study and prayer. Service on the session is the place where those who have already acquired such depth and maturity of faith provide leadership and guidance and sustaining nurture to those who have not yet been so blessed. Active service may afford a special, particular and/or greater opportunity for these things to grow, but that is an extra bonus to the servant, not a rationale for making a decision about the composition of the session.

And one more odd bit follows. The committee proposed an amendment, which was not sent down to the presbyteries. The proposal was to alter the description of business appropriate to a congregational meeting to include: *"...the session may seek advice from the congregation on matters of concern, with the congregation clearly understanding that the actions of a congregation my not violate the responsibility of the session as listed in G-10.0102."*

Now how did these folk who spent three years reflecting on our polity come up with the notion that we would qualify the role of the ordained officers' mandate and responsibility to govern with an occasional plebiscite, while reminding the congregation that the session was constitutionally bound not necessarily to pay any attention to their opinion! Needless to say there are ways to be in conversation with the congregation far less destructive.

Section E - Presbytery

The next section of recommendations had to do with the presbytery.

<u>Number 1</u>: to "encourage presbyteries to evaluate their size, both geographically and/or number of members, to assure that they are small enough to strengthen fellowship and enhance the decision-making process of the presbytery, and large enough to accomplish a viable common mission." Or, as they say at the local community bank, "small enough to know you, big enough to serve you" - except we are to be serving others, or so it would imply in the ordinary usage of the words "common mission".

In the early years of American Presbyterianism the constraints of the transportation system kept the geographic size of presbyteries to a minimum in most of the country. A presbytery consisting of 20 to 30 congregations would have been quite typical. Distances were manageable and minister members came to know each other. When the pastor of my youth died in 1958, the presbytery carried out the funeral service and virtually all the members of presbytery (about 25) were present and robed for the celebration. My first call was in St. Paul, Minnesota (just St. Paul; Minneapolis was still its own presbytery) and there were maybe 27 congregations. The ministers would get together for potluck suppers in members homes and a goodly percentage of us with our spouses, could attend comfortably in that intimate setting.

Then it came to pass that the 1972 re-organization mandated larger presbyteries, sufficiently large as to pay for staff and carry out the "common mission" "that can most effectively and efficiently accomplish it at the level of jurisdiction nearest the congregations" (most recently at G-9.0402b) The old Boards and Agencies were gone, consolidated into the Agencies of the General Assembly and coordinated by the General Assembly Mission Council (not the one we have now but the one we had then). What used to belong to the national entity now belonged to a governing body that could most effectively and efficiently (left undefined) oversee that work based on being closest to the work itself. One result was that presbyteries expanded their understanding of themselves as programmatic rather than ecclesiastical entities. Considerations of what one should be and do came to center on funds and staff sufficient for this mission now within the body's responsibility.

As the lines were being drawn to create these larger presbyteries criteria for viability were circulated. In the evolving Synod of which I was a part at the time these criteria included such things as a concentration of population; institutions of higher learning; airports; television and radio "media markets"; and other such socio-economic measures. And, of course, there should be enough membership in the congregations so as to generate *per capita* contributions sufficient to maintain the administrative structure for this program.

By 1993, at least in the former northern stream, these larger presbyteries had been in place for almost 20 years. For good or ill, it was apparent that larger bodies needed to delegate authority and responsibility to smaller bodies. Councils and committees were being granted broad powers to act on behalf of the governing body. The understanding that ruling and teaching elders, deliberating as a council of the church, that is, <u>the presbytery,</u> came to be diluted as more and more activity rested with sub-units or staff. The "business" of presbytery amounted to hearing reports of what others were doing, or had already done, in our name.

The continued decline of membership and re-direction of funds over the past 20 years has only intensified the concern. At the denominational level staff portfolios came to be broader and broader. In vast areas of the geography declining membership and resources have rendered presbyteries incapable of carrying out much that is required to be viable in any meaningful sense. Constitutional requirements are passed over or assigned to sub-units for responsibility and action.

<u>Number 2:</u> The report raised another concern that persists. Are the councils of the church beyond the session to be described only by geography? As noted before, the predominant character of the UPCUSA presence in the land of the Confederacy was a predominance of African-American congregations. At Reunion, the committee struggled with a solution to the obvious conundrum. If we maintained separate "black" and "white" presbyteries, we would perpetuate a cultural system we were opposed to, namely, implicit segregation. If the relatively fewer in number African-American congregations were put into presbyteries with the more numerous PCUS congregations, the autonomy and integrity of governance and esteem enjoyed by the African-American folk could be diminished. The solution was to affirm unity by declaring there shall be in this re-united denomination no "non-geographic" presbyteries and, there shall be structures in place to guarantee representative participation in leadership. (G-9.0104ff, G-11.000)

Nicely done! And, well noted and accepted as a good and sufficient resolution, until it was noticed that Dakota Presbytery, the oldest established presbytery west of the Mississippi River was a non-geographic presbytery established by and for Native Americans. It was right around the time of the reuniting Assembly in Atlanta that this reality came into widespread public view. And, coincidentally, at that same Assembly the ground was laid for the first Korean-American, non-geographic presbytery to be established. At the time of the Nature of the Church report the idea of a presbytery by and for Korean-Americans was already firmly established.

Perhaps to our sin and shame; the reality is that the great majority of us are of a Western European, rationalist/elitist, stripe and all that we say and do is reflective of the inherent cultural biases related to who we are. I acknowledge that, and I am not particularly inclined to apologize for it. That I try not to act out of the most destructive aspects of my biases is a goal I seek with no particular claim to uniform success. In other words out of sinfulness I work to create and participate in an institution that is itself "prone to evil and slothful in good".

So, "on the margins" of our life together, with immigrant populations and aboriginal populations, we allow and maintain non-geographic presbyteries. In the early years of this century aggressive steps have been taken to alter aspects of our Constitution to even more easily accommodate the unique cultural traditions of various immigrant groups. Still, among the African-American leaders within our denomination that I have worked with on the FOG revision process, the decision not to have racial-ethnic presbyteries and to mandate forms of participation was correct and must be maintained. Whether the folk in the pews of congregations that are not of the dominant culture believe that or not is something to be considered, by them, not by me.

The Nature of the Church report recommended that the Constitution be amended to acknowledge the existence of non-geographic presbyteries. It was and the current language of G-3.0403c reflects that. Over the intervening years many amendments related to this concern have been proposed. But the special committee on the Nature of the Church's proposed amendment was not approved and has not been addressed. That proposed section, on the responsibility of the General Assembly in regard to presbytery boundaries, would have added the words: *Ordinarily, presbyteries shall be of sufficient strength and geographical proximity to enhance the total mission of the church. Mutual counsel, support and sharing of worship and fellowship is encouraged in presbyteries whose boundaries overlap,* **with the eventual goal of the uniting of all in geographic presbyteries**. [emphasis added]

What do we mean when we say that presbyteries are a fundamental form of being church? What are the common bonds of unity that bind us together in such an organized entity? How important is "mutual counsel, support and sharing of worship and fellowship"? Are boundaries just lines drawn on the map the way victorious Europeans created "nations" in the Middle East after World War I? These were hard questions in 1983 at Reunion. They have been difficult questions in the intervening years, as anyone who has worked with Dakota or the several Korean-American presbyteries can attest. And now there are those who are wanting to form non-geographic presbyteries based in common theological (some would say social/political) understandings.

The definition of a presbytery is simple: *Presbytery is the corporate expression of the church consisting of all the churches and ministers of Word and Sacrament within a certain district.* [G-3.0301] That is a standard and the most simple structural form to organize and maintain. Perhaps the strange Constitutional word "ordinarily" needs to be inserted, although I would not like it. Rather the challenge is to do the work necessary to bind in mutual counsel, support and sharing" those within a certain district. To encourage, support and "direct" this work may be the most critical function that could justify the continuation of that council of the church known as the Synod.

<u>Number 3:</u> The third recommendation sought to add "polity" to the list of required exams in the sequence leading to ordination.

These were the recommendations in regard to sessions and presbyteries. All in all there was not much there in the way of specific interventions or correctives. But the issues dealt with have persisted and the need for change only increased. Do I believe that revising the Form of Government miraculously solved these concerns? Absolutely not. Do I believe that a document of Foundational Principles, clearly described and readily accessible gives the Holy Spirit material to work with in seeking solutions? Absolutely YES. Do I fear that not requiring unnecessary uniformity will lead to destructive "local option"? No more destructive than the chaos of the current reality. Do I think there is any hope for principled Presbyterian governance out of and within our tradition? YES. Sessions will seek the Will of God for the congregation. Presbyteries can and will continue to develop within their bounds the mutual mission of the congregations.

Section F - Synod

In the American experience, faithful "Presbyterians" from the "old country" gathered together for strength and support in the barren land to which they had come. In time these gatherings morphed into congregations with pastors. In time a presbytery was organized to regularize ministry and protect congregations from error. When the geography required multiple presbyteries, a synod was organized. As multiple synods were appropriate the initial General Assembly was convened to oversee all that had evolved out of the needs of those who gathered to pray and praise in the Presbyterian fashion.

But what of the synod now? The question was a lively one for the Nature of the Church committee. They shared the report of the General Assembly Committee on Review (1992)"that the role of the synod is not clear to most Presbyterians." An organizational chart of our governing structures most clearly puts sessions and presbyteries on the same level (or at least in the same realm) as seats of original jurisdiction. These are the ultimate authorities as no officer can be chosen or removed, no constitutional change made, save by action at one of these representative assemblies. General Assembly and synod, on the other hand are derivative bodies created by the action of the several presbyteries. And, despite all the attempts of the last century to act as if we are a hierarchical organization, the Constitution has never been amended to place synods in a "chain of command" structure. Synods continue to be independently created and referential only to the presbyteries within their bounds. [Hence, special provisions within the Constitution needed to be made for the oversight of non-geographic presbyteries made up of congregations within the boundaries of more than one synod.]

In the former "northern stream" a plan and structure was put in place after 1972 that created the "top-down" hierarchy favored by corporatists. In the former "southern stream" power was more widely distributed and synods had unique mission functions and funding mechanisms. In the years immediately following reunion the "northern stream" pattern of funding dominated and organizational charts came to be drawn with the General Assembly at the center.

If the movie tag-lines of Jerry Maguire - "Show me the money"; and All the President's Men - "Follow the money", are to be believed, then the idealized picture of cash flowing throughout the church tells the story. In the post 1972 UPCUSA "Circulating Funds" was the term that described a pot of money defined by negotiations between and among presbyteries, synods and the General Assembly. Gifts from the folk in the pew flowed to the center and then back out to the synods and presbyteries so that the work of mission could be carried out through program and staff. Personnel policies were centrally described and recommended to "lower" governing bodies. The effect however was to create the perception that synod staff were funded by and extensions of the General Assembly, and presbytery staff was seen as personnel assigned as needed to the presbyteries.

That this system broke down upon implementation and never functioned in any "pure" sense is beside the point. By the time of reunion the seeds of its dysfunction had long since germinated. What "sprouted" from the germ of an idea was that presbyteries (and many sessions) very quickly recognized that where the money started was a good place to exercise control. The flow that was to maintain the circulation quickly came to be "managed" at the bottom rather than at the top. Synods (for the most part), caught in the middle of this intricate "dance around the dough", never really found a unique ministry or the access to congregations to seek funding. Even true believers in the system discovered that the system was doomed to failure. Synod program gradually deteriorated or was deferred to General Assembly or presbytery control. (Yes, I know there are exceptions.)

So what was left for synods in 1993 - and still today? What is left is that which, if we did not have synods we would need to create some structure to fulfill. The UPCUSA prior to 1972 and the PCUS prior to 1983 had similar lists. Taking the PCUS list for example: The synod has power: to provide for administrative and judicial review (appeal); to review presbytery minutes and redress that contrary to order; to observe the Constitution and obey the injunctions of the higher court; to carry out such work as to expand and edify the presbyteries and sessions within its bounds; and to propose to the General Assembly such measures as may be helpful to the whole church.

In other words, a synod exists to oversee the presbyteries, to tend to appeals and respond to complaints against presbyteries and to carry out such a program of mission and ministry as its presbyteries necessitate. The days when General Assembly or its programmatic units would mandate and fund some mission or ministry and assign it to a synod(s) is long gone. Presbyteries within a synod's bounds could be called together to shape areas of mutual need and agree to mutual solutions and some have and do. The Nature of the Church report proposed several alternatives to deal with synods. Perhaps those proposals are as valid now as then. It's just that the Constitution has no interest or stake in such negotiations beyond the assigned functions of administrative review.

Section G - General Assembly

The Nature of the Church report proposed no Constitutional amendments regarding the General Assembly, *per se*. They did however direct attention to the Manual of the General Assembly. The Manual is a document that is approved near the opening of each General Assembly meeting. It contains procedural rules for elections and committee work. It contains material that guides the meeting itself and it also contains materials that direct how the offices (OGA and GAMC) function in the periods between Assembly meetings. A careful review of the Manual is an interesting study both for what is included and what is not.

The primary focus the special committee put on the Manual concerned "Advisory Delegates". Beginning around 1970 (at least in the northern stream) the practice was established of inviting each presbytery to send a "Youth Advisory Delegate" to the Assembly. The age range of these delegates has fluctuated over time. Currently they are designated as "Young Adult Advisory Delegates" or YAADs. From the beginning, or over time (I could research this but it's irrelevant) categories of Theological Student, Overseas, and Ecumenical Advisory Delegates were also included in the Manual of the General Assembly. These "advisory" delegates were granted the privilege of the floor; in committee meetings they were also granted the right to vote.

As there was no requirement that these advisers be ordained elders, and (with a possible rare exception) by definition they were unlikely to be Ministers of Word and Sacrament, we are already in a position of clouding the foundational principle that governance in the church resides solely and exclusively in the hands of presbyters, teaching and ruling elders, that is, members of ordered ministries. It could be and I suspect was argued that the privilege of voice can be granted to anyone by the body, and since committees are not authorized to take any official action the granting of vote in committee does not compromise our polity. So be it.

To those who watch the General Assembly regularly, however, things had gotten out of hand. They had gotten out of hand in 1989 when the study was begun. For the most part the TSADs, OADs, and EADs took their advisory role quietly. They were likely to speak only on matters that directly concerned the reason they were present. TSADs were wisely aware that ordination exams were yet to come and tended to keep a rather low profile. (In addition the numbers of these delegates was relatively small.) But the YAADs were another matter all together.

From the beginning the YAADs were housed separately from the commissioners. Advisers, counselors, chaperones (call them what you will) were assigned to the 'encampment'. It was in a way like summer camp with a polity theme. Speakers addressed the youth, they elected officers, they 'caucused' on the issues, they stayed up late at night eating pizza and doing what young people would be expected to do. For many of the early years a special section of seating on the Assembly floor was assigned to the YAADs. In practice, with unlimited access to the floor, this group became a real-time lobby, able to develop an agenda and organize response to floor debate "on the fly". In those early days voting was more cumbersome and the issues on which the YAADs wished to advise the Assembly were negotiated in advance or were called for as an exception, in other words, not every vote required advice. Even so, the presence of this organized group concerned folk and at some point they came to be seated with their presbytery delegations (although dilution of the YAAD's power was not the officially stated reason).

The special committee report proposed that the role in governance of these advisory delegates be scaled back. The report asked that the rules be changed to grant the privilege of voice in committees but without vote and that both voice and vote be removed from the advisers on the floor of the General Assembly. Needless to say, the largely emotional argument around hearing the voice of youth has carried the day. The proposed changes were not and have not been made.

The role of the YAADs continues much as it was in the late 80's. To those of us who watch most every Assembly it is a matter of concern that in committees it is often apparent that the youth have an organized presence within the committee. Materials shaped by them in their "caucus" or more likely in recent years shaped by one of the "interest groups" and passed through the hands of sympathetic delegates, are brought to the committee and presented. Every General Assembly will have several youth assigned as there are 170 some of them and something under 20 committees into which they are distributed. In plenary it is not uncommon to have the only persons speaking to an issue, or the vast majority of speakers, be from the YAAD category. Yes they are the best and brightest of our young people. Yes, they likely have read the material more thoroughly than the commissioners. Yes, they are better informed by adult advocates as to a wider context. But, still, in the deliberations of a representative assembly of presbyters, the deliberation is often solely in the hands of those who are not eligible to deliberate save their membership in this invited group.

The other part of the report's concern with advisory delegates had to do with just how many of them there are. Each presbytery is entitled to one YAAD. Give or take that's about 170 of them. The other advisory categories likely generate another 30 or so folk. So, when the standing committees are populated and when the plenary sessions meet, there are about 200 advisers participating. In committee, that's about 13 advisers sitting with about 55 commissioners (getting into the range of almost 25%).

The number of ordained presbyters, named as commissioners by their presbyteries, is proportional to the number of members on the rolls of its congregations. In other words, when we were a larger denomination there were more commissioners sent to the Assembly. With the decline in numbers the number of commissioners fell apace. At the time of the 1993 report the committee asserted that the percentage of advisory delegates participating had risen from 17 to 35 percent. I presume the period covered was from 1983 to 1993. Surely, in the years after 1993 the gap could have only widened. That meant that prior to going to biennial assemblies (and actually including the first biennial assembly in Birmingham) more than one of every three seats was occupied by an advisory delegate.

This disparity was pointed out during the debate to move to Biennial meetings and rather than accept the 1993 recommendation and adjust the number of advisers downward, the action taken was to increase the number of commissioners upward to re-establish the proportional representation at the time of Reunion.

There are times when I can see the weary faces of the Special Committee on the Nature of the Church and the Practice of Governance through the haze of their report. Words and sentences were undoubtedly haggled over. An attitude and mood of positive change was desired. I'm sure no one wanted to be portrayed as the grumpy old curmudgeon who just wanted to take us back to the "good old days". But every so often there is a breach opened by exhaustion and something like this slips through:(speaking of the value of the experience for the YAADs)

If this experience is necessary or vital for as many as 170 delegates, then why not increase the number of delegates so that more youth may participate? The fact is, there are more effective and less expensive ways to train youth in the work of the church, or to provide experiences for them in the life of the church, that do not affect the purpose and function of the General Assembly.

Over the past 50 years a number of YAADs look back to their General Assembly experience as a life-shaping one. Many, perhaps even a majority, have grown to serve the denomination in significant ways. Take that as a given.

Then again, there have been others. One year the commissioners of the presbytery I happened to be serving at the time looked daily for the smiling face of our young adviser; Where was he? Messages were left here and there. The group photo for YAADs was scheduled and he did not appear. Other YAADs did not know him. When we returned home and the commissioners made their report to the presbytery we heard the rest of the story. It seems that one of the first nights he had wandered into a cafe and a waitress had befriended him. She knew the scenic areas around the host city and was more than happy to entertain him. He had spent most of his time during the Assembly in the company of a local waitress and he was more than excited to share with the presbytery what a grand opportunity the church had provided him! [As they say, you cannot make this stuff up!]

I know that story is a gross, shameful and unacceptable EXCEPTION to the presence and the practice of having advisers. But the Assembly did not miss his advice and in that regard it likely does not and would not miss the advice of the majority of its advisory delegates in the future.

Section H - The Book of Order

I chose to begin with the report of the Special Committee on The Nature of the Church and the Practice of Governance, submitted to the General Assembly in 1993 because it was a convenient mid-point in a half-century of Constitutional change and consideration. That special committee was given a complex set of concerns to address and they developed an appropriately diverse set of proposed changes and emphases. It was the very last recommendation in the Report that was in fact the most comprehensive - REVISE THE BOOK OF ORDER.

Here is a rather extensive quotation from the recommendation:

The Special Committee on the Nature of the Church and the Practice of Governance recommends that the 205th General Assembly (1993) direct the Moderator to appoint a General Assembly Special Committee to Revise the Book of Order. The special committee shall review and make recommendations about **condensing** *the Book of Order,* **reducing procedural and regulatory provisions** *allowing* **greater flexibility** *in responding to the needs of the people of God, and shall* **emphasize that which is foundational.** *The foundational portion of the Book of Order is not to be amended easily and will require a two-thirds majority vote of the presbyteries to ratify. Such a committee would be charged to follow the recommendations of the Special Committee on the Nature of the Church and the Practice of Governance as amended and affirmed by the 205th General Assembly (1993)* [Emphasis Added]

In the implementation portion of the recommendation the request was even more specific:

The (new) special committee is to make clear those provisions of the Book of Order which are foundational; those which are policies and therefore binding on all governing bodies; and those which are guidelines and therefore advisory to governing bodies.

The direction given reflects clearly the charge that motivated all subsequent efforts and parallels closely the resulting revision. Is it any wonder that some (myself included) fumed more than just a little bit when speakers stood before the Assembly Committee in 2008 and argued against the draft revision as a somehow recently ginned-up idea by a cabal of General Assembly staffers working to ruin the church! (OK, those weren't their exact words, but I was hardly a disinterested listener!)

---

[1] While I know it has been done in at least two presbyteries, a "first" occurred at the 219th General Assembly in Minneapolis (2010). An infant received the sacrament of Baptism. Keeping with a theme established by John 7:38, that flowing water came from the believer's heart", it was determined by the planners that a renewal of the baptismal covenant was appropriate and an actual baptism would lift this theme. The baptism was authorized by the session of a particular congregation, a congregation that moved it's Sunday morning worship into the opening worship of the Assembly. Curiously, either out of concern for propriety or of oversight, the General Assembly itself voted to include the baptism (noting the session authorization) in an early vote. Just what approving that one aspect of an already planned worship service meant in light of the vows and covenants appropriate to the sacrament is a matter for speculation.

Part II Revise the Book Of Order

Chapter Six: The Early Years

It is...important to acknowledge that the Book of Order is being used more and more in a regulatory fashion to require uniformity as a test of purity. Our understanding of the nature of our being is one of richness, diverse expressions, and a variety of gifts that calls us to be able to respond in many ways. By stating who we understand ourselves to be in our Constitution and by implementing our principles through the use of manuals, we come closer to providing unity without requiring unnecessary uniformity. It is wiser to allow rules to be local expressions in conformity with fundamental principles than to require that there be a vast number of rules covering every possible situation.

This paragraph from the Special Committee's rationale sets the agenda for what became a 17-year pursuit. In late 1992, as the report was being drafted, the committee focused on the entire Book of Order. In subsequent years, both the (now titled) Directory for Worship and the Rules of Discipline have been completely revised and approved by the presbyteries. The task was finally completed in 2011

The Rules of Discipline tell us just what to do when all else fails. No one sees them as defining us. Although when we read of church fights in other denominations and wrong-doing being dealt with in unjust ways, we might want to suggest that Presbyterians have a just and agreed upon way of doing things. But, the reality is that only a few Presbyterians, in practice, ever look at the ROD.

The Directory for Worship is a fine and articulate theological statement of the comprehensive scope of spiritual practice in the life of the Christian and how that spiritual awareness can be portrayed in both individual and communal settings. However, as implementation of the spiritual life is entirely within the discretion of the pastor and session, the Directory finds little need for many specific directives. The style and content of the Directory are such that just about anything can find a place. In an environment where anything is permitted there is little point in referring to or fighting over the content.

But within that quotation from the report we find exposed why the pursuit of revision took so long. It is the matter of addressing language that prescribes behavior. We have cherished our prescriptions.

When it comes to following our answers to the ordination questions, the vow to pursue the "peace, unity and purity" of the church is a favorite. Here we have a piece of meat we can sink our teeth into. Peace is important and we even have a "department" in the programmatic structure to pursue it; but a vast minority if not a majority of Presbyterians prefer to see the flow of that list backward. "My desire, to be like Jesus", we sing lustily. Recalling that Jesus said, "Be perfect as your Heavenly Father is perfect", we seek to engender among us a church that is PURE. We cling to the standards of our ancestors. When we are CERTAIN THAT EVERYTHING HAS BEEN DONE BY THE BOOK, then we will be UNITED, and united we will be at PEACE. It is that sequence that many implicitly believe they promised to "further" upon ordination.

Contrast that with the special committee's statement that it is "wiser to allow rules to be local expression in conformity with fundamental principles than to require that there be a vast number of rules covering every possible situation." Can it be possible that foundational principles could be so well understood and accepted that sessions and presbyteries would make decisions that are in the vast majority of cases completely in keeping with who we are and what we claim to be? Cynics and skeptics argue that this would not be the case. While they do not say it, they convey an implicit message that others cannot be trusted, therefore they must be restrained. It is the sophisticated and elitist Presbyterian version of the old cliché: "There is no one righteous save me and thee, and sometimes I'm not certain about thee."

I give credit to the Special Committee for its recommendation and to the countless numbers of commissioners through the intervening years who said, "We trust each other enough, to pursue this revision and to seek the resolution recommended back in 1993"! I celebrate all those across the church who voted – finally – to make the change. I believe history proves the "purity-seekers" wrong. Presbyterians have lived faithfully for a long time with very few of them carrying the rule book tied in a booklet on their forehead or strapped to their wrists.

Laying Down The Path

As is most often the case; when presented with a major report, the General Assembly received the material and acted on virtually none of it. The matter of revising the Form of Government was referred to the Advisory Committee on the Constitution (ACC). This presented a bit of a problem, but an unavoidable one.

The ACC was created because those who shaped and formed the Reunion of 1983 distrusted strong authority in the Office of the Stated Clerk. Why this was true is beyond my ability to recount save speculation, but that it was true, is true. It had to do with "interpretation". Prior to reunion, if you wanted to know what the Constitution meant, and you felt you couldn't figure it out yourself, you contacted the Stated Clerk, and received an (the?) answer. Reunion drafters, for whatever reasons, did not find that satisfactory. The ACC was created to fill this function of interpretation. Elected by the General Assembly these folk would comment on every proposed constitutional matter "going up" to the Assembly and, when asked, render interpretation of what the existing text meant. Opinions and advice offered by the ACC was subject to confirmation by the full Assembly. In essence, only the Assembly could interpret the Constitution. There was no thought that the ACC would be itself a programmatic or action inducing entity.

But now it was handed this mandate, Revise the FOG. In addition, buried in the papers of the Special Committee was a "ham-handed" outline of what this revised document would contain. Whole chapters of existing text were sorted into "foundational" material on the one hand and "policy" material on the other.

David Meerse was a member of the ACC and took up the task of responding. He crafted a document reflective of the directive and circulated it widely among Stated Clerks and polity wonks across the church. It became evident very quickly that the task of discerning what material fit in which category was more complex than a simple sorting of paragraphs into various piles of text. The sorting itself had implications far beyond any division. The ACC reported back to the Assembly that the charge required a different kind of effort. The Assembly, in effect, said, "Try again!"

The efforts were slow but the task inescapable. Anxious not to over-step and frustrated with its progress, the ACC convened a working group to refine the definitions. In October of 1996 a meeting was convened in Chicago. William P. Thompson, John Pharr, Marianne Wolfe, David Meerse, Margaret J.Thomas (at the time Moderator of the ACC) and I worked through clarifying the definitions. Utilizing a metaphor of parallel civil structures, we spoke of the United States Constitution, federal legislation (the "law of the land") and departmental rules and procedures.

Thus was born this set of definitions:

Foundational Material *contains the concepts and principles that have developed throughout the life of the Presbyterian Church (U.S.A.) as a part of the Reformed tradition. It emerges from the theological, philosophical, and historical experience of the community to become the symbol of the covenant to which the members of the Presbyterian Church (U.S.A.) adhere. As such, it is the essential basis for our common effort in ministry and the guide for our relationships with one another and with those outside our fellowship. It constitutes the point from which our future aspirations are projected and is therefore essential to the continuity of our mission.*

Binding Policies *are those policies that apply the "Foundational Principles" from which they derive and to which they are subordinate. The general welfare of the PC(USA) and the universal applicability of the binding policies to the fulfillment of the church's mission requires the voluntary submission of members and officers to them and their enforceability by more inclusive parts of the church governing bodies and officers.*

Advisory Practices permit the whole church to seek unity without requiring uniformity. In addition to such advisory material currently in the Form of Government, the General Assembly will approve administrative procedures intended for churchwide application. When such procedures relate to General Assembly functions, they shall be binding upon the General Assembly, but advisory to other governing bodies. The General Assembly should maintain and publish a compilation of current procedures. Other governing bodies may approve such advisory procedures or initiate procedures of their own.

In 1997 the General Assembly received these definitions and directed the ACC to proceed to craft a revised FOG based upon them.

In July of 1997, a month after this action of the Assembly, the Advisory Committee on the Constitution met by conference call to choose the task force to carry out the assignment of turning definitions into revisions. Criteria for selection were primarily related to experience as a stated clerk or service as a Judicial Commission member. Of course, diversity and geographic considerations played a part. The result was a task force composed of the following people:

Convener: Neal Lloyd, Pastor, Rock Island, Illinois, former presbytery Stated Clerk and Interim Executive Presbyter; Catherine Borchert, Stated Clerk, Presbytery of the Western Reserve, Cleveland, Ohio; Barbara Campbell-Davis, Executive Presbyter, Presbytery of New Hope, Rocky Mount, North Carolina; David Meerse, Stated Clerk, Presbytery of New York City; Richard "Deke" Spierling, Pastor, Leonia, New Jersey, Judicial Commission experience; and Sun Bai Kim, General Assembly Council staff working with Korean-American ministries. (Dr. Kim accepted the invitation but was never able to participate in the work.) C. Fred Jenkins, Associate Stated Clerk for Constitutional Services of the Office of the General Assembly served as staff.

Over a thirteen-month period between September 1997 and September 1998, the task force held four face-to-face meetings. Writing assignments and circulation of working drafts continued between meetings. The work in progress was submitted to the ACC in January of 1998 and again in March of that year.

The claim "that one does not want to watch sausage or legislation being made" did not apply to this process. While there were strenuous debates and countless re-writes of the material (what sometimes seemed to be the most trivial of points), the team worked well together and the work proceeded smoothly.

One anecdote from the process is reflective of the commitment of the team to the task. Kitty Borchert had broad and deep experience in both governance and judicial work within the church. She had followed this process closely and her desire to serve was strong. A week or two before the first meeting she contacted me to say that her husband's cancer had progressed to the point that he had been admitted into a hospice program. She feared she would be unavailable. I commiserated with her sorrow and disappointment and urged her to keep me informed. Early in the morning of the day before our first meeting my secretary transferred a phone call, saying that Kitty was on the phone. I knew before I picked up what that message would be. Frank had died early that morning. We shed a tear and shared a bit of the sorrow, and then Kitty said, "I'll be in Chicago tomorrow. He knew how much I wanted to be in this work. I may not stay for the whole meeting, but I'll be there."

She came. We prayed and we sang and we sorrowed, and then we went to work. At lunch on the day she was to leave us, through a mistake, 6 extra lunches had been prepared for our group. The management said that nothing could be done to correct the error. "Kitty," we asked. "You'll have a house-full when you get home, why not take this food." So, she got on the plane for Cleveland with six large Cobb Salads in Styrofoam containers in her carry-on! The man next to her on the plane indicated he was quite hungry, having missed his lunch; so she gave him one! The rest went to her children as they shared their grief.

At the conclusion of the September 1998 writing team meeting the document prepared was finalized and submitted for consideration by the General Assembly. That Assembly, the 211th met in Fort Worth, Texas in 1999. It would be fair to say that the document delivered into the hands of the commissioners was somewhat beyond the comprehension of the commissioners.

Fort Worth – 1999

"I was only doing what I was told", is, of course, the defense of the morally lazy. But, when directed by the General Assembly to take the existing text of a document and re-craft it into three distinct and clearly defined forms of language, I will confess that I do not construe that as a license to be creative. And thus, I suspect, our first effort to re-fashion the FOG was un-creative. We carefully tracked each paragraph and sentence in the existing text (as have all subsequent efforts). We did not want to stand accused of changing the Constitution through editorial "trickery". Yet, to conform to the needs of the English language, certain "openings", "closings" and "transitions" needed to be added. Where concepts were less than clear, some editing for clarity may have taken place. But, when we arrived at the Assembly the commissioners saw a document that was cumbersome, hard to handle (physically as well as intellectually) and strange to the eye. What the document was not, was new, or a change, or in some way a surreptitious attempt to re-shape or reform the church.

For those unfamiliar with the way material is dealt with at the meeting of the General Assembly; every item of business goes first to a standing committee composed of elected commissioners and advisory delegates assigned to the committee by random selection. The matter is brought to the table and those advocating for it, or arguing against it, are given an opportunity to speak. If it is a Constitutional matter, the Advisory Committee on the Constitution offers its advice. Then the commissioners debate, discuss and decide.

After their initial presentation, unless called upon, the creators/advocates must sit quietly and listen. As this work had been a project of the Advisory Committee on the Constitution itself, the advocacy/advice piece was combined.

To be perfectly honest, I have virtually no recollection of the debate. I had led a task force to do a task and we had done it. I am sure the debate and discussion was extensive. I don't think it was dishonest, rancorous or mean. But it was also clear that there was no way this document was going to be approved in whole or in part. As things progress in committee deliberation an observer can tell when the momentum is moving favorably. Amendments are offered and either approved or denied, comments are relevant and to the point. The "energy" in the room is active, engaged and seeking to yield a clear response. I can't say that any of that happened.

On the other hand, commissioners do recognize that people have worked hard to produce material for their consideration. They don't like to say "no". There are always some who want to offer something that can be approved. In the end, the General Assembly was presented with and approved a motion thanking the ACC for the effort and directing that the Foundations section become a piece suitable for the website. As I recall it would have cost $3000 to print copies for each session but only $600 to put it on the web. You can guess the primary motivation involved in the decision. (And don't quote me on those numbers, I truly do not recall.) From 2000 until 2006 one could find on the Office of the General Assembly website a document titled "Foundational Principles of Presbyterian Governance."

Thus, the first full-blown attempt to re-cast the FOG came to an end. Looking back, that is a good thing. The task force carefully reviewed each chapter, paragraph, sentence, phrase and word and re-crafted existing text into one of the three categories. Usually that was easy, sometimes it was difficult. As highlighted earlier in this history, issues of justice, diversity and standards led individual members to hold certain passages in different categories. But, the product was an effective fulfillment of the charge.

On the positive side, by displaying material in three parallel columns, it was easy to see how a foundational value flowed over to a binding policy which then was applied in a piece of advisory information. But visually the narrow columns and large amounts of white space was an unattractive distraction and led to an excessive length.

The Next Phase

That might have been the end of it. But the effort to serve the Constitution by stopping the flow of "manual of operations" amendments and changes in practice that ran contrary to foundational principles did not abate.

Hope springs eternal, but frustration is a good motivator also!

The 212th General Assembly convened in the Long Beach Convention Center on June 24, 2000. Here the final nail was driven in the coffin of the Advisory Committee on the Constitution's attempt to fulfill the desire of the Special Committee on the Nature of the Church and the Practice of Governance Report and create a re-formation of the Form of Government. It was in Long Beach that the inexpensive and perfunctory action suggested the year before was approved and the Foundational Principles were posted on the web as a "study document".

In reality the need for revision was only intensifying. Out of frustration and the constant barrage of questions and problems put before the Office of the General Assembly's Constitutional Services Department, the following request was put before the 212th:

The decision of the 211th General Assembly (1999) not to proceed with a revision of the Form of Government prepared by the Advisory Committee on the Constitution, left unanswered a number of questions raised in recent years regarding the length and complexity of the rules and procedures, and a widespread feeling that there is too much unneeded detail. Early in January, the Stated Clerk met with three synod and presbytery executives, two staff members from Churchwide Personnel Services, and two staff members from the Office of the General Assembly to consider what would be a useful method for a renewed effort to address the concerns.

It was agreed to focus on Chapter XIV - Ordination, Certification and Commissioning, since that chapter is the one most often mentioned in complaints about rigidity and complexity. General Assemblies from 1995 through 1999 received forty-three proposals to amend sections of Chapter XIV. an additional ten overtures seeking to amend the chapter are on the docket for this year.

What the Stated Clerk then proposed was a condensed version of the chapter in question. Stripped of much procedural detail, the Assembly was asked to circulate this draft widely across the church for comment and response prior to the next Assembly. The draft sought to remove procedural detail, condense and summarize basic principles and rules, and make the document more flexible without making substantial changes. As a statistical point of interest it was noted that the then current text of chapter 14 contained 15,203 words and the revision 9,596.

The request contained this critical caveat: ...it is not clear how much liberty the church is willing to give to the presbyteries and congregations in matters concerning church officers and commissioned or certified persons in ministry.

Ah, the threat of liberty!

Of course the presbyteries, sessions and congregations already were exercising their liberty in all kinds of ways. When presented with a rigid procedural manual embedded in the Constitution, an inflexible set of procedures that could not be fulfilled or the fulfillment of which amounted to tending to the "deck chairs" on someone's idea of how the Titanic ought to sail; folks were making up their own rules or ignoring them with impunity.

Take only one example: Fred Jenkins, the Director of the Office of Constitutional Services would observe that when he had been received into the UPCUSA from the United Methodist denomination there were only two titles that applied to the way in which a minister was related to a congregation. One was either a pastor (including Associate and Assistant Pastors) or a Stated Supply. In other words, a congregation either called a pastor or the presbytery sent a pastor. In the mid-nineties, when we would discuss this, his count was that the Form of Government now specified 19 titles that were Constitutionally defined.

On the one hand, the "hard law of lists" thus required that if a presbytery thought of a new title that would fit a particular ministry, a Constitutional amendment would be required; for when there is a list, that which is not listed is not permitted. (The logic is that if the Constitution wanted that title it would include it.) How cumbersome! On the other hand, because of a plethora of titles, the appearance was that one could just "shop from the list" for something that seemed to apply. The Constitution defines pastoral positions as "permanent" and "temporary". Seeing the word "temporary pastoral positions", at least one presbytery approves pastoral service under the title of "temporary pastor". I don't know if the Latin phrase *"reductio ad absurdum"* applies, but certainly such chaos is absurd!

The Assembly chose to circulate the draft revision of Chapter XIV for discussion.

In 2001 the draft of a condensed version of Chapter XIV was once again placed before the Assembly. This time the Stated Clerk could report that the draft had been circulated around the denomination, suggestions had been incorporated and it was recommended to be sent to the presbyteries for their affirmative or negative votes. The commissioners agreed (after tweaking it in several places to suit their taste) and it was sent down.

By now, if you have been following closely, the rationale for such proposals have become familiar, the phonograph record (remember those) stuck in the groove and repeating over and over and over again – simplicity - flexibility - clarity. Fortunately, because we are "creative" writers, each rationale strikes some new ground, coins some new phrase, pens some yet un-uttered wisdom in hope that this time, this time it will be heard. The Stated Clerk wrote (in part):

The above proposed revisions of the Form of Government seek to ground our churches(sic) ordering of ministry in the theology and polity of the Reformed tradition, while making the procedures for ordination, certification, and commissioning more flexible. The basic principles followed in the revision were as follows:

1. The theology of ministry found in the Book of Confessions *and the foundational principle chapters of the* Book of Order *encourage us to keep the polity dynamic rather than static.*

2. The theology of ordination in the church was not under review, so all changes were focused on procedures and processes, not on fundamental change.

3. The changes were designed to allow greater flexibility to governing bodies, particularly presbyteries, in providing for ministry in their congregations. Specific standards and procedures will be adopted by governing bodies, with guidance from advisory handbooks developed by the entities of the General Assembly, as directed by the General Assembly.

The debate in the presbyteries was intense. Opposition was heated and sufficiently similar across the church as to at least hint at formal organized opposition. The finally tally reported 29 presbyteries in favor; 141 presbyteries opposed and 2 voting "no action". What could account for such an overwhelming rejection of a matter that had been in the purview of the denomination for a decade? There was one primary issue that carried the vote. Could an Interim Pastor become the next installed pastor of a congregation?

Interim Pastors as Organized Lobbyists

The Alban Institute was formed in 1974 (that seems late, but they say it on their website) and some of its earliest research focused on transitions. Studies on how ministers move from seminary to parish ministry and from one congregation to another. They also studied how a congregation deals most effectively with the transition from one pastor to another. Their work identified certain "tasks" that made such transitions more effective and useful to further the ministry of both pastors and congregations. "Interim Ministry" arose as a specialty out of such research.

In 1987, Alan Gripe (a denominational staff member) published the first edition of a Manual for Interim Ministers. Subsequently, the Association of Presbyterian Interim Ministry Specialists was organized. The proposed changes in Chapter XIV of the FOG allowed a presbytery, by a 2/3 vote, to allow an interim pastor to be called as the next installed pastor. The organized interim ministers opposed this possibility and "intentional" interim pastors spoke against the revision at virtually every presbytery meeting assembled to vote on the revision.

There was a smattering of other concerns; the most intriguing one had to do with the questions asked of officers, commissioned lay pastors and certified workers upon their transition to office or place. In the existing text, at each place where a transition occurred, the questions to be asked were fully listed, even though all but one of them was identical in all instances. The proposed solution was to insert a section in the Directory for Worship (since all such events are to take place in the context of worship) and list the basic ones once and then the unique ones with appropriate designations. This change would have the double benefit of saving space and reinforcing the concept that ordination, installation and commissioning are acts of worship.

In many places there was opposition and to summarize the argument, "we need to keep the ordination questions in the Constitution!" No amount of indication that the Directory for Worship was, indeed, in the Constitution was able to dissuade the objectors. "No one would ever think to look in the Directory," they retorted. And so it was that some presbyteries voted "no".

In 2002, because hope does spring eternal, St. Augustine Presbytery asked the Assembly to send it out again, this time with language altered to specifically state that Interim Pastors could not succeed to the called position. Other forms of temporary supplies could still succeed by the two-thirds vote; and, with the questions put back in the Form of Government.

The Assembly directed the Office of the General Assembly to study the matter again to determine just why the last proposal was defeated! The Office of the General Assembly sought to clarify and solidify the direction of revision. Using the Office of Research Services and every event where governing body staff and elected folk were gathered, the proposal to revise was discussed, tweaked and polished.

By this time the move had been made to hold meetings of the Assembly only every other year. Thus, the polity plate of the 217th General Assembly (2006) came to be heaped with the question of revision. Out of the consultative process a "new", better just say, "another", comprehensive revision of Chapter XIV was considered and approved to be circulated to the presbyteries for their affirmative or negative votes. This time the vote was a close (89 for, 83 against and 1 no action) but positive affirmation is still positive and the revised Chapter XIV came into the Constitution as of June 2007. For the curiosity of the matter; the ordination questions did end up in the Directory for Worship (W-4.4000) and an Interim Pastors were not allowed to be the next permanent pastor in that position.

Chapter Seven: The Current Book is Born

However, the 217th had a bigger fish to fry. The matter of a comprehensive re-casting of the entire Form of Government was still raised up as a definite, if not a crying need. The "push" came from several places. Recent immigrant fellowship groups; new forms of congregational structure; "emergent church" theology; and large numbers who come to Christ with no church experience; all perceived the FOG as more hindrance than help. Presbyteries and sessions needed the flexibility that had been sought for all these years.

And so, a Task Force was commissioned.

In consultation with the GA Nominating Committee the 2006-2007 Moderator and the past two General Assembly Moderators selected nine persons. The TF was to include among its number: at least one Clerk of Session, one session Moderator, one new immigrant pastor, one executive/general presbyter, one Stated Clerk, one Committee on Preparation for Ministry member/staff, one Committee on Ministry member/staff, and one member of the Advisory Committee on the Constitution. By the end of the Assembly the Moderators had done their work, the Task Force was named and the date of the first meeting was established.

Why the rush? An amendment from the floor had added a condition that the work be completed and circulated to the whole church by September 1, 2007. That left only 14 months from the conclusion of the Assembly to complete the work. The Task Force met in the first week of August 2006, and completed its work by late August of the next year. (I say that because the material was not actually posted on the web and printed in hard copy until after September 1, and some attacked the product at the subsequent Assembly as having been "late" and hence the church was not given adequate time to study it.)

Between specifying the makeup of the TF and giving a fixed time-line for the work, there were five descriptive assignments:

1.   The New Form of Government (nFOG) shall preserve our foundational polity (perhaps most concisely laid out in the first four chapters of the current Form of Government).

2.   The focus of the nFOG shall be on providing leadership for local congregations as missional communities.

3.   The presbytery shall continue as the central governmental unit, as it has been throughout most of our history. The nFOG shall provide sufficient authority and flexibility to allow the presbytery to assist congregations in addressing the changing cultural, economic, and societal challenges in our new millennial world. The FOG Task Force shall take notice of and address the institutional and structural impediments that currently cripple so very many of our presbyteries.

4.   The nFOG shall provide flexibility at all levels, granting authority while permitting governing bodies to develop the structures to carry out their respective missions.

and, in light of recent work and concern, number 5 sought to guide the TF in its manner of doing its work...

5.   The FOG Task Force shall be guided by the principles proposed by Recommendations 1-4 from the Theological Task Force on Peace, Unity and Purity of the Church, using those principles as a guide for its own processes and deliberations. They shall incorporate this new Presbyterian ethos into the Form of Government so that it truly functions as the Presbyterian Church (U.S.A)'s guidebook for missions.

Within the group that came together in August of 2006 to follow the GA mandate to revise the FOG, (Once again I felt called to volunteer and was privileged to be chosen to be a part of one of the finest groups of persons I have ever encountered in my years in the church.) I believe each one of us had a clear sense of who we were and why we had been chosen. The opening round of sharing was frank, straightforward, and even generated some awareness of the personality-traits each of us brought along with our expertise. The diversity within the group meant that the demands of both ardor and order would be held forth. No one was timid, no one held back.

Because the mandate to the nominating process directed that certain "staff people" (Stated Clerks and Executive/General Presbyters are "elected" officers, but they mostly function like "staff" members) serve on the Task Force, it was determined to be less than wise to place any of them in positions of leadership on the Task Force. As the Task Force included six Ministers of Word and Sacrament and three Elders, and as one of the Elders was a staff person, it was decided that the two "normal" Elders be designated as the conveners. Cynthia Bolbach of Arlington, Virginia, and Sharon Davison of New York, New York, shared the leadership.

In addition to becoming familiar with each other and our task, we spent the first meeting clarifying just what might have been meant by the charge as it filtered from the Office of the General Assembly through the minds of the commissioners. We also developed a reading list of contemporary scholars who are wrestling with what the state of the denominational church is in our society. Not to forget our heritage we committed to read again Part IV of Calvin's "Institutes" on the nature of the church.

As the work progressed over the subsequent 13 months most of our decisions were the result of collaborative discussions and consensus was easy to arrive at. When we did "vote" they were typically a perfunctory confirmation of material we had worked long and hard to hone and perfect. When "sticky wickets" were encountered we stopped and gave opportunity through the practice of "mutual invitation" for all to be heard before any decision was made.

<u>To preserve and revise</u>

 As we came together and sought to outline our task, as is the case with every General Assembly entity or task group, the first step is to place clearly in view **just exactly what did the Assembly ask us to do**. There we began our work.

The New Form of Government(nFOG) shall preserve our foundational polity (perhaps most concisely laid out in the first four chapters of the current Form of Government).

This is an interesting juxtaposition of words. The "new" FOG shall "preserve". What were we to make of the first four chapters of the then current Form of Government? How deep is the purported affection the church holds for them? Let us be brutally frank. This beloved document was at the time 25 years old; that is long enough to breed familiarity but hardly a patina of antiquity.

Chapter One had perhaps the strongest claim to preservation. This collection of "declarations about the nature of the church (Christ the Head and the "Great Ends") and principles of governance trace their roots through some of our binding strands, back into the earliest days in America. The appended (or so it would seem) definition of just what it is that is included in our Constitution seems patched to the end and would likely appear as an "add-on" wherever it appeared.

Chapter Two affirmed that we are a "confessional" church. In earlier Constitutions this material was not necessary. The Constitution simply included THE CONFESSION, that is, Westminster. Once we acknowledged that many confessional streams came together to form and shape who we had been and what we professed to be, this chapter became foundational. As the concept of a "book of confessions" originated in the Northern Stream in 1967 we may give this material a 40 year presence in our self-awareness.

Chapter Three reflected on mission. (In light of what came to the Task Force in directive number two, one might ask what is wrong with this statement, but more on that later.) Since no Christian body can avoid Christ's "Great Commission", the notion that we should even have to declare that we are on a "mission" seems redundant. But, in the 1960's and 70's leadership perceived that the pews had become complacent, comfortable, frozen. An emphasis on mission became the order of the decade and theological statements clarifying the outward-looking, other-directed nature of our life together were shaped to under-gird the challenge. This chapter reflects that emphasis and call. Give this one 50 years of "heritage".

Chapter Four was really two chapters, one on unity and one on diversity. The twentieth century saw idealism and necessity alter the picture of American Protestantism. On the one hand Christ's High Priestly Prayer that "all may be one" compelled us to seek common faith and action with other believers. The concilliar movement was spawned of this. On the other hand the post 1960 decline in denominational strength led to efforts of cooperation and mutual recognition among our faith-partners. The "unity" section gave us our self-understanding to engage in these relationships.

Diversity, quite frankly, is a post 60's emphasis. Whether we were or were not diverse previously is not the question. What is surely true is that we had not determined that highlighting the differences that existed within the whole was important. And therein lay the problem. Raising diversity to a discrete Constitutional status highlighted differences within the body. Yes, the Apostle Paul used the different gifts metaphor to describe the Church, but he used the metaphor to strengthen the unity not emphasize the differences. While helpful in homiletic activity, metaphorical language in a constitutional document can become problematic.

Finally, in the middle of those "beloved" first four chapters, stood another list of principles of governance. Why was it not up in chapter one with the others? I guess it was just not old enough.

Anyway, this cherished, treasured and highly commended encapsulation of foundational principles, while being true and good and familiar was, in the opinion of the Task Force, neither old enough to be sacrosanct nor sufficient as a comprehensive written document to be preserved. It as determined to make the attempt to use this material and shape it into a more helpful document without sacrificing the principles.

Directive number two read:

The focus of the nFOG shall be on providing leadership for local congregations as missional communities.

The FOG Revision Task Force had to wrestle with the charge given us by the General Assembly to focus the Form of Government into a "leadership document" that will move congregations to be "missional".

First off, a Constitutional Form of Government describes and prescribes entities and processes. It is, and needs to be, to as great extent as possible, neutral as to outcomes and goals. The extent to which outcomes and goals are embedded in the forms and structures is the extent to which the document can be seen as a manual of operations or in worst cases a blatantly political document advocating for a particular opinion within the body. As the Apostle might say, if I spend too much time protecting the ear, the eye is bound to feel excluded and get upset. Better to just say there shall be a head and require that ears and eyes be attached to work out for themselves just what they shall see and hear. Each entity can determine for itself who its leaders shall be and what causes shall be mutually agreed upon, the document itself merely describes the framework within which they operate.

Then there is the focus on the congregation. Now I will be the first to allow that the core existence of the church, its essence is brought into being by God at those places where persons who seek to be faithful come together in assembly to worship, praise, and witness. There is no church without a congregation(s). But, our polity is not organized around congregations. With very limited exceptions, congregations are not governing entities in our tradition. Over my lifetime one of the greatest insults that could be delivered in ordered debate is the charge that a speaker or a proposal is "too congregational". Congregational polity is held in disdain by all right thinking Presbyterians.

Our prayer is that those who lead in our denomination, teaching and ruling elders - will lead the whole people into faithful witness. That is our 'confessional' goal and purpose. But the FOG is a book related to how we govern ourselves beyond descriptions of our mere existence. We govern ourselves through representative bodies of presbyters gathered in sessions and presbyteries (and synods and GA). The Task Force was challenged by what approach and emphasis on congregations could be fulfilled while preserving the polity.

And then there is that word "missional". Its been a long time since I wrestled with the grammar books at the level of determining what adding a suffix does to a word. I know that adding "al" to "region" produces an adjective that indicates the noun is being contextualized by reference to a geographical area surrounding it. Adding "al" to "person" speaks of the context around an individual as "communal" references a group. So what context does "mission-al" add to "communities"?

The congregation is the community of reference, and its mission is to be in its context. But is that something new? Does our polity suddenly become a "missional ecclesiology" as if it has not been thus before? "Go ye therefore into all the world" was the first stated purpose, has it been supplanted? Does it need to be brought up from some antiquarian vault as if it is some kind of Dead Sea Scroll only recently discovered by a wandering Bedouin? Only a generation ago we labored under the banner that "Everything the Church Does Is Its Mission". We re-structured our governing structures "for mission". Mission was no longer to be done "over there" but was the business of right here, just outside our door. That some folk may find that our witness is inadequate to the time, that God's people are still ensconced in their "comfortable pew" is not the fault of our rhetoric or our labeling.

Anyway, we wrestled with this sentence. We read the writings of theologians and practitioners who talked about what it meant to be a missional community. We held these concerns as we shaped the language that began with what it meant to be a member of the church, a faithful follower of Jesus Christ. We held on to the work of God among us through Christ as we sought to describe how sessions and presbyteries worked. Was it possible for us to create some unique and new document and yet one that would bear sufficient resemblance to our heritage that the church might accept it? Those were the challenges.

Directive three said:

*The **presbytery** shall continue as the **central governmental unit**, as it has been throughout most of our history. The nFOG shall provide sufficient authority and flexibility to **allow the presbytery to assist congregations** in addressing the changing cultural, economic, and societal challenges in our new millennial world. The FOG Task Force shall take notice of and address the institutional and structural impediments that currently cripple so very many of our presbyteries.* [emphasis added]

I suspect in Calvin's Geneva and Knox's Scotland there were a multitude of necessities that led to something that could be remembered in the New World and described as "The Presbytery". Certainly the inheritance of a geographically delimited ecclesiastical units called "parishes" and "dioceses" was chief among them. Whether for management reasons or simply for the constraints on travel and communication, the notion that the Church of Jesus Christ (the entity spoken of in Biblical terms as "The Body Of Christ") would encompass each and every gathering of believers as a particular congregation was universally applied. In America, as our heritage evolved, that overseeing entity came to be called the presbytery.

The presbytery saw to it that every congregation had leadership and that those available to be approved as leaders were theologically sound and appropriately trained. Further, each presbytery reviewed the work of the congregation by overseeing the minutes of its session. Administrative review was, in theory at least, about the quality of pastoral care and teaching and not about citing the page number that demonstrated meetings were opened and closed with prayer.

Through the late 19th and all of the 20th centuries there arose, and came to dominate, a perception of the denomination as a national entity like unto a great secular corporation. Programs were generated at a national level and "marketed" out to the presbyteries, sessions and congregations. Ideas and values were reflected upward into national structures through commissioners and elected board members. Cultural influence at the national level was taken for granted, as cultural rights were granted to mainline churches in discussing matters of ethics, morals and national policy. The problem was we never altered our Constitutional understandings so as to remove the presbytery from its place of prominence. Because synods and General Assembly are derived from presbyteries; and because no significant change can be made without a majority of presbyteries approving;

the perception of a strong, centralized, corporate, national church setting standards and enforcing behaviors was always a misunderstanding of our polity.

Do not be mistaken; there is a strand of historical understanding that could argue for describing the denomination as a centralized entity. These can be defended in the monarchical understandings of both the Scottish and the Westminster traditions. It's just that we never wrote the Constitution of this denomination to reflect that understanding.

Now we find ourselves in an era when the influence of the denomination on the national cultural scene has withered to irrelevance. And, we find ourselves in a situation where that cultural irrelevance is reflected in the understandings of many of our pastors and people who find the more inclusive governing bodies and even the Constitution itself to be a burden and a hindrance in doing the mission they see Christ calling for. Like it or not, the reality is that in settings of rapid change, in communities where immigration is changing the "face" of those we see daily, in places where new Christians outnumber those trained-up in the traditional denominations; in more and more places around the country the reality is that our notion of a centralized, Constitutionally-controlled church is indeed a hindrance to the mission of Jesus Christ.

So, the charge to the task force implied and directed that if we were to preserve our unique Presbyterian heritage it would only be by reinforcing the place and authority of the presbytery such that it could be saved. For that to happen presbyteries would need to be granted a great deal of authority and flexibility to shape and craft work and witness reflective of our historic and foundational principles. Such work will not and cannot look the same in every place. Such forms, or more precisely the absence of nationally standardized forms, might be risky. Serious and pastoral administrative review may need to occasionally place a check on innovation. But the "one size fits all" polity that can be so comfortable and that is desired by so many is a burden that will sink us.

Directive number four read:

The nFOG shall provide flexibility at all levels, granting authority while permitting governing bodies to develop the structures to carry out their respective missions.

Back in 1996, when the Advisory Committee on the Constitution shaped definitions to guide this task. The framework for understanding utilized as a metaphor the secular distinctions between constitutional, legislative and administrative directives. But what I recall most clearly from that meeting were the words of the late William P. Thompson as he reflected on the Federalist Papers and the early Supreme Court decision of Marbury v. Madison. To review:

Federalism and The Federalist Papers in the period of the American Revolution and the days leading up to the adoption of the Constitution encouraged the establishment of a strong central government. Others feared such a concentration of power out of their direct experience of unchecked monarchical authority. The political compromise that led to final ratification of the Constitution included the immediate amendments that are known as the "Bill of Rights". These rights described constraints on the power of that central government. The tenth amendment is perhaps among the broadest of these constraints. It reads: *The powers not delegated to the United States by the Constitution, nor prohibited by it to the States, are reserved to the States respectively, or to the people.*

This will sound a note in harmony with the phrase that appears in the Form of Government at F-3.0209 *Councils possess whatever administrative authority is necessary to give effect to duties and powers assigned by the Constitution of the church. The jurisdiction of each council is limited by the express provisions of the Constitution, with powers not mentioned being reserved to the presbyteries.*

In our Form of Governance, this statement of "General Authority" is preceded by this statement in F-3.0206: *A higher council shall have the right of review and control over a lower one and shall have power to determine matters of controversy upon reference, complaint, or appeal.*

This was the struggle in the early days of the American Constitutional experience, that is the power of "review and control". And this is where *Marbury v. Madison* comes into play. The matter that was at issue is of little significance, but the principle it established in 1803 came to be foundational to our nation. Marbury had petitioned the court for redress of a grievance. In its decision the Court declared the statute under which he claimed redress to be unconstitutional. This was the first instance where the Supreme Court declared the legislative action of the congress to be unconstitutional. While review of this sort must be used with extreme caution (lest an impasse make governance impossible) we watch in our own day as judicial review continues to be used to keep (we pray) the executive and legislative branches within the bounds established by the Constitution.

The parallel structure in Presbyterian practice in the Form of Government provides for both Administrative and Judicial processes. G-3.0108 and .0109 summarize these values and practices. Of course the Rules of Discipline provide another complete set of practices for resolving differences and addressing complaints.

So what do we do with a mandate to *provide flexibility at all levels, granting authority while permitting governing bodies to develop the structures to carry out their respective missions?* The authority in question was already clearly granted. Presbyteries and sessions have always possessed original jurisdiction. Synods and General Assembly have authority derived from the presbyteries by virtue of their own constitutionally assigned responsibilities. The only significant change in this regard was to eliminate mandated lists of structures that each presbytery must have. The numerous functions each council is mandated to fulfill are serious. Not being given a structure is not a license to shirk responsibility. In the new reality the review of a council goes forward without the burden of each council having an identical structure. What is critical to this flexibility's success is the review. Higher councils must take this seriously, both administrative and judicial review, as well as the awareness that some review will and must require reproof and correction. Flexibility cannot function without review.

Conclusion

Everything that has happened since 1989 led to where we find ourselves. The work proceeded the way God's work through the church has always proceeded; by means of the halting, feeble, very human exercises of God's Spirit in community. Each start, each stumble, each victory and each defeat nudged and prodded.

Did the drafting Task Force come together with a firm hard grasp of either the "task" or the "product"? I don't believe so. We picked up our assignment and looked at what had gone before and what had been asked for. Then we prayed, and talked, talked and wrote, re-wrote and prayed some more, challenged and confronted, shared laughter and disagreements. In the end, words appeared on paper and we said, "this is what we were asked to do, it is the best we can put forward, it is faithful to the past and open to the future."

We sought to preserve the foundational understandings in Chapters 1 through 4 of the current book. But they were taken apart and re-formed in a new way. We consolidated the Form of Government and placed it within a framework provided to the Church by the Nicean Creed and the 16th century Reformers' understandings of where the Church is to be found. Without a doubt we agreed that this material belonged in its own special section of our Constitution. It is not better or of greater worth than other material. But we do believe that it is important as a resource for teaching and as "grounding" in why it is we affirm the more directive and prescriptive issues related to governance.

The Foundations and FOG sections affirm that governance is a unique and "peculiar" emphasis in our Presbyterian heritage. Yet these are not the WHOLE Constitution. It is only a part and material contained elsewhere is equally available and necessary.

The current FOG focuses attention primarily on the work of congregations as exercised through the session and on the work of presbyteries as they oversee those called into service as Teaching Elders among the congregations. For this emphasis to function each council must have the flexibility to interpret the foundational principles in its own setting. Mandatory forms and functions are reduced to a minimum such that work and witness may be unimpeded by over-controlling rule.

For that to succeed two things must be recalled. One is that we are engaged in a mutual mission shaped and directed by God's Spirit, a mutual enterprise in which trust in each other is essential. The second is that administrative and judicial review are real and expected ways in which we hold each other mutually accountable for our actions. In "olden days" this review focused much more on theological understanding than on behavior. We need to return again to some sense that discussion within the councils of the church about our theological assumptions is likely of greater importance than our review of a particular programmatic thrust or the potential behavior of a candidate for ordination. That we continue a pattern established at our very origin, a pattern of maintaining openness to diversity of theological view and allowing councils to determine what is and is not essential in matters of faith, is implicit in the revision.

Part III: A Brief Overview

Chapter Eight: A Review of the Foundational Section

Part of me would leave the summary overview of the FOG out of this book. For the most part, those who write let the writing stand for itself and leave commentary to others. Lord knows there are more than enough critics in the world without critiquing one's own work.

The basic theological/ecclesiological position of the Constitution remains unchanged. The Book of Confessions stands as a summation of our principle understandings about faith and life. The Book of Order is a derivative and more narrowly focused document seeking implications and applications of our faith tradition. The Foundations and Form of Government sections are not intended to capture a fully integrated, comprehensive, theology of the life and practice of faith.

One point of some interest that readers may overlook is found in the footnote at the beginning of the Foundations section. It has to do with the use of the capital and lower case letter "c" in speaking of C/church. When I was growing up I was taught that the Universal Church, the Body of Christ, Church, the BIG Church was always capitalized while the particular church, the church of a congregation, the neighborhood church was always small lettered. I can't say I recall how the denominational church was treated in those days. In recent years I know that editorial conventions changed and, frankly, I have been inconsistent and often read inconsistent usage in this matter.

The Task Force determined a pattern for our own work that reflected what we believed to be true about the place of the Presbyterian Church (U.S.A.) in the cosmic scheme of things. For our purposes, the BIG C Church is still big and we, we the denomination, are little. This is reflected in the statement in F-1.0402, *The presbyterian system of government in the Constitution of the Presbyterian Church (U.S.A.) is established in light of Scripture but is not regarded as essential for the existence of the Christian Church nor required of all Christians.* It is further reflected in G-1.0101, *The congregation is the basic form of the church, but it is not of itself a sufficient form of the church.*

We are, in our manifestations of faithful living in community, derived from Christ who is the great Head of the Church. We are his and not our own. Even though the experience of American Presbyterianism may be construed as having been created out of the actions of faithful men and women choosing to affiliate within the Reformed heritage; all of our affiliations and covenants are derived from the Covenant of God in Jesus Christ calling men and women of faith into Christ's Church. That's the really big C.

So that language might be clearer, the Task Force chose then to describe a local gathering of folk simply as a congregation rather than the previous nomenclature, that is a "particular church". Some saw in this decision a move to describe only the denomination as a "small c" church and hence demean congregations in favor of the denomination. Certainly that was not the intent and there is nothing of substance in the FOG to support that assertion. If ultimate authority resided within the purview of the General Assembly a fear of abuse of power could perhaps be justified. But, as power ultimately resides in sessions and presbyteries, even if the use of capital and small letters mattered, there is no inherent threat that results from either consistent use of capitalization.

When the proposal was approved for submission to the presbyteries the Assembly chose to amend the footnote spelling out this use of capitalization. The more complex usage was taken away and only the convention of a capital "C" Church meaning the Church Universal/Eternal remains.

A theological framework

"History of Doctrine" was a required first year course in 1966 when I began study at Pittsburgh Theological Seminary. We began with the post-resurrection Biblical material and worked meticulously forward, adding layer upon layer of nuance to the core of Peter's affirmation, "You are the Christ, the Son of the Living God." In the second year we were required to take Systematic Theology. The faculty and/or trustees required that the class be taught according to tradition. So, we began with the Doctrine of God, expounded as the Church has expounded it through time. Several years later, in a summer course I was introduced to the concept that the Primary Metaphor one uses to begin a theological reflection absolutely determines the way that theological reflection must unfold itself. Change the central metaphor and you change the theology. The beginning point is important.

I likely never was, and certainly am not now, a superb theologian. I confess that the finer points and more highly nuanced understandings either escape me or do not catch my interest. I am content to live with a degree of imprecision. But I am aware that the contemporary world of Church life displays great variety within the discussion of what could be labeled Christology. Who was Jesus? How was He the Christ? What did He do? Why does it matter?

Within the culture there are great numbers of believers who begin their understanding of faith with Jesus as the principle metaphor. To live in faith is to follow Jesus, the "pioneer and perfecter". As the Task Force wrestled with the challenge to revise the FOG out of a missional perspective it was determined that the existing initial metaphor – that Christ is the Head of the Church – be prefaced by a prior declaration that the Triune God initiates the action by sending Christ into the world.

Why? An answer from my seminary days might be that the Nicean formula of the Trinity, the great anchor-point for faith, is essential to who we are. Virtually everything we do that matters is set in the context of a recitation of the Trinitarian formula. The Trinity is our link to Christians around the world. That is who and how God is. A second, more contemporary answer is that the missional theology we were to reflect begins with the sending act of God. The "action" out of which faith grows is not fundamentally the action of the Incarnate One in whom we see God, but rather the act of God in the sending of that Incarnate One. God is a God who inserts God's-Self into the world. God initiates.

Therefore the Triune God now is central to the initial paragraph of our Foundational document. (F-1.01) Do not let this detract from the former first paragraph which now stands second, that is the claim that "Jesus Christ is the Head of the Church".(F-1.02) Christ's Headship stands in a context of God's prior action, the action of the Triune God, beyond time and space, who has called into being the Church which is One, Holy, Catholic, and Apostolic. As the Form of Government is about the life and work of the Church and more particularly our church, PCUSA, this principle metaphor rests upon the full exposition of faith contained in the Confessions but it is put forward as a sufficient basis on which to rest the polity of the church. [Note: I have capitalized words according to my preference and not in keeping with the document itself in every instance.]

Diversity and inclusion

The Reverend Dr. John Maxwell Adams was my mentor. He had retired from a career serving ministries in higher education and worshiped with a congregation in what we called, in those days, the "inner city". The hulking old building, built in the "Gilded Age" of the nineteenth century easily accommodated the 70 or so worshipers in its 450 seat sanctuary. Small in numbers, yet what a fascinating assemblage it was. There were some white folk who had left the neighborhood but not their church; some poor white folk who had nowhere else to go; and then there was a wondrous rainbow of people from various races and clans who now lived nearby. Max used to say, I attend there because I believe it looks like what the Kingdom of God will look like!

What are we to say in our official Constitutional documents to cast the Will of God for the Church in those terms, when, in practice, we are an overwhelmingly Caucasian, overwhelmingly well-educated, upper middle-class, affluent, and comfortable denomination? In earlier years our Constitutional statements were less complex and quite straightforward. "The universal Church consists of all those persons, in every nation, together with their children, who make profession of the holy religion of Christ and of submission to His laws".[1] Who is included? What part of "all" don't you understand?

The cultural context, out of which our current Constitution arose, however, demands more specific language. The struggle for civil rights and the battles waged in the denomination to end the legacy of discrimination makes anything less than an outright declaration of inclusivity seem to be a step backward.

Two innovations in the 1983 Constitution sought to prevent this. There would be no "non-geographic" presbyteries, presbyteries segmented by race. And, there would be within each presbytery a mandated Committee on Representation, the composition of which was strictly prescribed, charged with the task of holding the presbytery accountable to include in its life and work the full diversity of its membership.

The final sections of Chapter One of the Foundations seeks to move our understanding of openness and diversity from a culturally bound description of categories of persons and rigid structural responses, to a strong assertion of what we believe, belief we claim to be foundational to our practice. At core, it says that our unity in Christ leaves no room for discrimination against any person. The guarantee of openness to all concerned some folk sufficiently that striking most of this affirmation was suggested to the Assembly. But the assertion stands as a description of a long term view of the existence of Christ's Church inclusive of a more fluid understanding of what we mean by "all persons".

Two concepts come to the fore. One is the assertion that while we believe that our particular denomination is established in light of Scripture, it is not essential to the existence of the Church nor do we assume that all Christians will agree with us. A bit of humility before God is helpful. The second grows out of the mandate to reflect a missional theology. Everything we do is to seek to follow the working of the Sovereign God's mission in the world. A series of phrases close out Chapter One, each indicates that we "seek: a new openness...." The search for what God is already doing in our world, and the flexibility for all entities of the church to seek it, is a foundational understanding on which the provisions that follow in the Form of Government rest.

Continuity after change

Describing a separate "Foundations" section required this new phrase to be inserted:

F-3.03:

The statements contained in this section, "The Foundations of Presbyterian Polity," describe the ecclesiological and historical commitments on which the polity of the Presbyterian Church (U.S.A.) rests. Provisions of any part of this Constitution are to be interpreted in light of the whole Constitution. No provision of the Book of Order can of itself invalidate any other. Where there are tensions and ambiguities between provisions, it is the task of councils and judicial commissions to resolve them in such a way as to give effect to all provisions

The first sentence states the obvious; these foundational principles are the "ecclesiological and historical commitments" on which our polity rests. What follows is where some have become concerned.

In recent years, and as a part of what made the revision desirable, many people have focused attention so exclusively on the Form of Government as to forget, neglect or ignore other parts of our Constitution. It is critical to keep in mind that our Constitution consists of TWO books, one containing 11 parts and one containing 4 parts. Underlying all of these written documents stand the Scriptures of the Old and New Testament as they have been accepted by the church. When a question arises within a congregation or one of the councils of the church and an answer is being sought, the discernment process is not complete until the entire treasury of church wisdom has been considered. Merely looking in one of the documents for a word or phrase or sentence or paragraph that gives "ammunition" to support our pre-determined view is not sufficient. This second sentence is intended to remind readers of the Foundations of polity that the field of vision is broader than any one document.

The third sentence addresses a question that came up early in the revision process. In the report of the Nature of the Church and the Practice of Governance Special Committee it was suggested that once Foundational material was determined and segmented such material should be elevated to a status within our Constitution equal to the material in the Book of Confessions. In all subsequent discussion such a possibility was considered, but then dismissed.

Two arguments led to the determination not to seek such an elevated standing for this material. The first is a rather arcane legal assertion that to take existing material and try to elevate it would be to argue that amending certain material would require a larger majority of support than was required to approve it at the time of its initial approval. I take that to be the argument that only something akin to a "constitutional convention" could make such an alteration. The second argument is much more mundane. In the current culture of suspicion in our life together, there is no need to seek such an elevation. This thinking also explains the decision not to seek an extended period of years during which the Foundational material could not be amended as was proposed at one time.

These two considerations led to this sentence as a reminder, however, that the Foundational material is a part of the Constitution equal to all other parts. No one part "trumps" any other. In real world terms, when a council is drafting a "manual provision" for governing its life, it will reflect upon ALL sections of the Book of Order, and the Confessions, and the Scripture in seeking the Mind of Christ for the Church.

The final sentence is thus made necessary by the three preceding. For what do Presbyterians do when the result of study, reflection and discernment do not yield a satisfactory answer, or an answer seen as faithful by all? Well, we provide for routine administrative review of one council by a "higher" or more inclusive council. And, we provide for judicial review when necessary.

Has the approval of the proposed revision resulted in the negation of all judicial decisions and Authoritative Interpretations made in the past. If we had never revised our Constitution before, perhaps such a concern could be valid. However, we have revised our Constitution and it has not disrupted our tradition of interpretation. Interpretations rendered in the past apply to that portion of the Constitution that is the same as, or most clearly similar in intent to, the portion previously addressed. Precedent is still precedent. If indeed there is material that is so innovative as never to have been seen before in the history of our communion, then new precedent would need to be established. To reinforce this perspective a special committee was chosen to report to the Assembly the status of all previous interpretations. The overwhelming majority of which are easily sustained by the current text.

---

[1] The Constitution of the Presbyterian Church in the U.S.A., Form of Government, Chapter II, section 2, 1914 edition. And I expect those words go back farther than that, that's just the earliest edition I have at hand.

Chapter Nine: A Review of the Form of Government Section

What is a congregation?

_Identity - Authority - Relationships.

For reasons that have been explored earlier, the Form of Government begins not with the abstract considerations of Christ's Church but with the very particular considerations of a gathered congregation of believers. Current literature, in both secular and religious media, has pretty well written off the "established" churches of what was once called the "mainline". Even Roman Catholic identity has suffered in this transition to what is typically labeled as a "post-" something world.

Those of us who have clung to the inheritance of the Presbyterian presence in American society have watched our numbers dwindle, actually cascade downward. The rational explanations and rationalizations have not been satisfying. And, as we have watched our own numbers decline we have seen the proliferation of the "independent" congregations, the "community" churches. We now are able to see emerging networks of such congregations gathering around the leadership of particularly dynamic and large congregations. The "Willow Creek" network and the "Saddleback" network can easily define a "community" of congregations whose leaders have followed the instruction and inspiration of Bill Hybels and Rick Warren. As I look at it, I can easily project myself as an assistant to either king or bishop in the mid-1500s and describe a similar scene for those congregations that had aligned themselves as followers of the teachings of Calvin or Luther or Zwingli. Indeed, we may be witnessing the rise of a new denominationalism.

So be it.

But we are where we are and who we are and we seek to shape defining statements that make ourselves clear. The effort to revise the Form of Government was not an effort to re-shape or re-make ourselves into something we are not. The answer to those who wish to be something else, to be bound by other vows, guided by other principles is to go where such vows bind and principles guide. We choose to affirm principles and practices that have sustained us. However, aware that the gathered community that is called a congregation is where the church is most obvious and where most members believe the church to exist at its most fundamental level, the FOG begins with the congregation.

The most critical section, to my eye, is G-1.0103:

A "congregation" as used in this Form of Government refers to a formally organized community chartered and recognized by a presbytery as provided in this Constitution. Each congregation of the Presbyterian Church (U.S.A.) shall be governed by this Constitution. The members of a congregation put themselves under the leadership of the session and the higher councils (presbytery, synod, and General Assembly). The session is responsible to guide and govern the life of the congregation. The session leads the congregation in fulfilling its responsibilities for the service of all people, for the upbuilding of the whole church, and for the glory of God. Other forms of corporate witness established by the presbytery shall also be governed by this Constitution and shall be subject to the authority of the presbytery.

A congregation is "formally organized, chartered and recognized". This is a link to the Foundations section. Christ is the head and calls the Church (Universal) and the church (Presbyterian) to follow where He leads. But we understand that call out of a context of the "one, holy, catholic and apostolic" tradition as shaped by the Reformed experience. Each congregation is its own unique manifestation of Christ's Church. Yet it is possible that each and every member of each and every gathering of believers could propound the illusion that there is a direct and uninterrupted link between Christ's own call in Scripture and the existence and righteousness of their particular congregation. But we reject such a notion. Each congregation gains its identity from those who have gone before. Even if we start from scratch in a barren land, all that we have and all that we are as a congregation is borrowed from that stream of Christ's "Being" that comes to us when a presbytery of this denomination, under the authority of this Constitution declares that we are a congregation.

That is our identity. Out of that identity flows our authority, an authority that comes from our acceptance that God in Jesus Christ, calls and appoints and sets apart leaders to guide us. We submit to those leaders, presbyters members of ordered ministries. Within this order, these ordered ministers also submit to the relationships established by our Constitution. Councils of the church willingly offer up their faithfulness to review and the potential of correction by higher councils. When correction is offered or censure handed down it is accepted humbly as one lovingly being nurtured in faith.

At the extreme end of this (rather utopian) understanding is the responsible assertion that the "only grounds for schism is apostasy". I have worked with and respect those within our denomination who are deeply troubled by actions or teachings engaged in or endorsed by the councils of the church. I respect those who understand apostasy. Their agony with who we are is real and their acceptance of the binding nature of our relationship is consistent with our tradition. On the other hand, far too many have sought to claim a cheap and easy road to departure. They engage in civil litigation to seek a claim on church property. They seek to lead faithful members out of our denomination into some form of independency or a more friendly denomination. Motivation is not always clear and rhetoric is often shaped to their advantage, but the basis of their discomfort lies in their own determination that their identity and authority is no longer enhanced by the covenantal relationship they claimed in their ordination.

In placing their determinations over their relationships within the church; without being able to declare under the Constitution (the full Constitution, not just a few provisions of the Form of Government) that the church has abandoned Jesus Christ, its Head; they are wrong. We share with them the fundamental understanding that the congregation, a gathering of faithful followers, is at the very center of our concept of the church. But we assert that the congregation is that center only as it is recognized by and in strong relationship with the whole of Christ's Church. Otherwise it is not Presbyterian as our Constitution defines Presbyterian.

Membership

Was it Mark Twain, Will Rogers or Groucho Marx who said "I wouldn't want to belong to any organization that would have me as a member."?

As the congregation is at the core of what we mean by church, the determination of just who is a member is important. Of course in ancient days when there was no separation between church and state, everyone who lived was a member of the church. The Reformation in many places simply changed the sign on the door but not the reality of including all citizens as members. Even when post-Reformation reformers led people away from the established church, these nonconformists rarely lost their place on the roll of the established church, unless, that is, they were burned at the stake for their disobedience.

From my experience with the Scandinavian immigrant communities in the Midwest, I know that many of those who came to American fled their homeland because of religious dissent and the penalties that may have accompanied it. For such persons, membership in the community of those who shared a common faith was a critical mark of personal identity and of place in God's Kingdom.

On the other hand, our early forebears in several states established religion in the same way it had been established in the old country. In the early days of the Massachusetts colony the pastor was a civic official and the call to a pastor was approved by all the citizens, not just all the members of the village church. Throughout the 19th century more church attendees were likely to be adherents rather than members. Most of us are familiar with the pattern described for President Abraham Lincoln, who "rented a pew" at Washington's New York Avenue Presbyterian Church and kept his pew at a Presbyterian congregation in Springfield, Illinois although he was never a "member" of any congregation, at least during his presidency.

So what do we mean when we say member? We speak of the commission we receive in our baptism. We place the water on the head of an infant and we say to that child, "...you are now a member of the Body of Christ and marked as Christ's own forever." Then again we receive people on Profession of Faith and we ask them to vow that they will be a faithful member of THIS congregation and to be present with their time talent and treasure.

We live with these two functional definitions of "member" (professed/active and baptized) that are unrelated to each other in many ways. We are content (or at least adapted) to live with using the word in both ways. In practice at the congregational level we would best be served by focusing only on the members we call "active".

The material in G-1.04 is clear and concise. In the age when congregations reach out to people in so many ways beyond the hour of worship on a Sunday morning, when "constituents" may relate to the congregation through one of the social networks or by regular use of a podcast, or through a local access cable broadcast or radio ministry, or by dropping in midweek for a Bible Study or prayer time, our reach can far exceed the names on our roster. We might boost our self-esteem and simplify our life by seeking to count "adherents" while reserving the category of membership for those who have made public profession and continue to make regular and faithful use of the "means of grace".

Meetings

The final section of FOG G-1.00 describes "Meetings of the Congregation". Balancing the goal of flexibility against the need(?) to protect order; the section strikes a balance between urges to spell out in great detail exactly what should happen and provisions that specify little or nothing. Given our view of governance resting in the councils of those set apart for ordered ministry, the most critical section of the proposed revision is G-1.0503. Here all the matters appropriate for congregational consideration are preserved.

One phrase was not carried over from the previous FOG. The congregation may consider "matters related to the permissive powers of a congregation, such as the desire to lodge all administrative responsibility in the session,". This was one of those places where a long discussion occupied the Task Force, not on the deep implications of the substance, but on trying to figure out what the phrase meant in any setting. I can't say that we resolved it and perhaps some who find it necessary will present an overture at some point asking with clarity for its re-insertion.

The discussion of congregational meetings opens up the way(s) in which a congregation (in current language "a particular church") functions under the laws of the various states. The Constitution encourages incorporation of congregations and each state has its own requirements for how corporations must behave. In some states, congregations may even have choices as to what particular path to incorporation they may choose. The more detailed and restrictive measures of the current text may actually inhibit congregations or place them in some potential conflict with legal requirement or local practice. One change required immediate attention. As the FOG now leaves meeting notice and quorum requirements to the discretion of each congregation, many have had to quickly insert such provisions in their manuals.

Throughout the FOG it is helpful to pay attention to the phrase "by rule". We make certain assumptions in entrusting governance to representative councils, and other entities, that people are capable of enacting rules to govern the uniqueness of their own life in faith. That there be rules is essential. Rules are proposed, publicized, approved and followed. Rules can be reviewed in the normal course of accountability. But not all rules need to be identical. In many cases a congregation or a session determine what is best for them.

Leadership: ordered

 Chapter Two of the FOG is large and required considerable effort to wrestle through what in our practice of calling and installing people to ordered ministries and ordered service was essential and what was flexible.

Virtually everyone who might read this is aware that concerns about sexual practice had been the primary focus about fitness for service in ordered ministry for a generation. The culmination of this concern had likely occurred in 1996 with the insertion of the paragraph numbered G-6.0606b. The revision was barred from proposing an alternative although the current text has replaced the language with wording approved at the same time as the revision. In matters of addressing the character and conduct of potential leaders the text of 2.0104a (former G-6.0606a) has always granted sessions and presbyteries the authority to determine that a particular individual is engaged in a lifestyle or holds a belief that disqualifies that person from bearing office.

Indeed, with only the general descriptive language of paragraph "a" councils might be led to a broader view of what beliefs or behaviors put barriers in front of ordination than focusing exclusively on gender relationships. Following on, when an individual is confronted with the will of the body to bar access to ordered ministry, that person has always had available to them the means of grace implicit in repentance, forgiveness and the opportunity then to serve. In the current debate about same-gender relationships, it was not so much that any particular individual sought to elude scrutiny as it was the perception of a majority of the presbyteries that particular sessions or presbyteries were acting in bad faith that led to the insertion of paragraph "b", to seek control of such behavior. The attempt to control only led to contentious judicial processes and great uncertainty. Over the 15 years that "b" was in the FOG all that became clear was that no particular control resulted.

This leads to the expressed concern that what may be evolving in the life of the church is a "local option" in matters of ordination. The phrase is cast to the winds as an epithet. Alleging that all order and faithfulness will be abandoned should the notion prevail, opponents (or, if you like, the proponents of a particular type of faithfulness) seek to frighten people. The problem is that in decrying what they term local option they decry what is and has always been the foundational understanding that only sessions and presbyteries have the power to ordain and that authority is exclusive and inalienable and can be challenged only through administrative and judicial review.

The intensity of feeling on both sides of the debate around gender and sexual practice draws us to the footnote attached at G-2.0105. *"That when any matter is determined by a major vote, every member shall either actively concur with or passively submit to such determination; or if his conscience permit him to do neither, he shall, after sufficient liberty modestly to reason and remonstrate, peaceably withdraw from our communion without attempting to make any schism. Provided always that this shall be understood to extend only to such determination as the body shall judge indispensable in doctrine or Presbyterian government."*

Here is the coming together of the balance between the conscience of an individual and the cohesion of the group. Here is the foundational material for our refusal, over time, to lock down a set of "essential teachings" to which everyone must adhere. Here is the basis for the right to declare a "scruple" against a matter that may be determined to be non-essential. But here also is the provision that there comes a time when individuals who cannot live with the determinations of a majority must either sit quietly or leave. Of course there is no set timeline at which either the individual or the body may determine how long the period of "sufficient liberty" shall last. Still, our protests against the decisions that grieve our conscience have this parameter against which we are to live.

The particular ordered ministries

In a bit of an innovation this section places the ordered ministries of the church in the sequence of their evolution. As Deacons were the first ones set aside for service, and as early congregations were governed or overseen by elders, with offices of specific oversight coming later, the FOG places the ordered ministries in that sequence. The provisions for defining, electing, approving and ordaining Deacons and Ruling Elders are familiar. Provisions whereby these ministries may be laid aside or the authority of the church renounced are described uniquely to these ministries although the language is parallel to similar language related to Teaching Elders.

Teaching Elders are described in familiar terms. The material presented in G-2.0504 however does offer some new language and clarity. After the categories of membership in presbytery have been defined, categories described to accommodate various ways in which a person may retain the ordered ministry of Teaching Elder, the text shifts to define "pastoral relationships" as a specific ministry. This is what Teaching Elders do as pastors. As pastors, Teaching Elders are in relationships, in relationships with congregations.

Then we move to what types of pastoral relationships are available. There are two. That's it, only two. Teaching Elders relate to congregations either as 'installed" pastors or as "temporary" pastors. Installed pastors serve either indefinitely or for a designated term. Temporary relationships are those relationships that serve the congregation when there is no called and installed pastor in place. Here the presbytery has the responsibility to work with the session and determine a mission strategy most appropriate to the life of that congregation. Upon that determination any number of types, styles and titles of service assigned to either Teaching Elders or Ruling Elders (especially trained and commissioned or not) may serve the mission purpose.

What is the level of control that is to be asserted over the "sovereign" rights of presbyteries and congregations to make determinations as to leadership? If the right of a congregation to call its pastor is inalienable (G-2.0102) on what basis does the Constitution constrain that right? This is a question that has now been answered with a considerable degree of flexibility.

Past practice has felt it wise to rule that persons currently serving the congregation as an Associate Pastor or an Interim Pastor possess an unfair advantage in the deliberations of a Pastor Nominating Committee and, hence, should not be allowed to be called. The FOG still contains a paragraph (G-2.0504a) that says that an Associate Pastor "is not...eligible" to succeed to be the next installed pastor of that congregation and one (G-20504b) that indicates that one who has served in a Temporary Pastoral Relationship "is not ...eligible" to succeed to be the next installed pastor of that congregation. Section "c" that follows then describes how a presbytery, when its mission strategy permits, may, by a three-fourths vote, make an exception and allow such a call to take place.

Leaving the exception in as a possibility offers two challenges. The first is a challenge to the presbytery to determine a mission strategy in relation to its congregations (including the possibility that its mission strategy will never allow such exceptions). The second is the challenge to those who engage in intentional ministries of a temporary nature. These folk often claim an understanding of ministry that defines effectiveness in terms that absolutely preclude consideration of the temporary pastor as a candidate for the installed position. Fair enough. Then they must also determine ways to effectively communicate their understanding to the congregation in places where the presbytery strategy may allow it. Put in other words, current wording has determined that a prohibition should not bind the whole church for the sake of presbyteries who will not define a mission strategy, or as protection for Teaching Elders who (apparently) cannot adequately assert their own will?

An alert reader may have noticed in the paragraph above the three little dots between the words "not" and "eligible". What is missing is the word "ordinarily". Having worked long with the language of the Constitution the drafting Task Force knew that it is clearer to have mandates that are clear mandates. Words that bind, should bind and words that offer flexibility should say so. Putting a mandate next to "ordinarily" creates an opportunity for confusion. The drafting strategy was that if the Assembly did not wish to offer the church flexibility in these matters the "section c" material could be removed, leaving the prohibition intact. Unfortunately the Assembly added "ordinarily" instead. Hopefully, in practice, this word, ordinarily", will be seen as laying the foundation for the potential exception that follows. If not it could be the source of much confusion

Preparation for ministry

The Constitutional provisions governing the manner in which a person is prepared to be ordained as a Teaching Elder were until 2007 the most complex set of specific actions described in the Form of Government. The elaborate stages and steps by which a person proceeded from a session recommendation, through inquirer and candidacy phases to ordination were highly detailed. If anyone wanted a illustration of the meaning of "manual provisions" in the Constitution, this section was the best example.

The current text seeks to retain a uniform pattern of stages and steps without overly restricting the process. Stripped to this minimal structure something emerges that it seems many in the church have overlooked or wished away. Preparation for ordination to the ministry of Teaching Elder is entirely, emphasis, ENTIRELY, the responsibility of the presbytery. It is the presbytery that receives the recommendation of the session, acts to approve each stage of the process, nurtures the person throughout, decrees when requirements have been met and has the authority to waive any of those requirements.

Questions have been raised and some have challenged that the exact titles of areas of examination a candidate must complete in G-2.0607d have not been maintained. The perception is argued that since we say that the act of a presbytery to ordain a person as a Teaching Elder is an act taken "on behalf of the whole church", the whole church through its Constitution should precisely specify the expectations. The problem is that although the "standardized exams" have been the practice since the late 1960s, those exams have always been products of presbytery activity and not activity of the whole church.

This is a hair worthy of being split, for the situation is not as clear as some may wish. The examination process is under the direction of the Presbyteries Cooperative Committee on Examinations. They see to the preparation, administration, evaluation and reporting of the examinations. The staff person to this process is a staff member in the Office of the General Assembly and the General Assembly oversees the work of the committee, which is composed of representatives selected by the presbyteries through the "reading groups" as well as persons chosen by General Assembly to serve as members at large.

In the days before this process (It began in the "northern stream" in 1967 or 1968.) each presbytery examined candidates according to its own practice. Stories abounded of examinations lasting for hours, sometimes spread over more than one meeting. Some candidates received virtually no substantive questioning while others were grilled on the minutest point of theology. It seemed wise (and still does) that there be some minimum standard of examination that all candidates complete. Rigorous and sometimes grueling as the exams may seem to candidates, it is good to recall that they were prepared as a blessing to both the church and the candidates.

Yet even as this standardized system was prepared and enacted it was maintained with absolute clarity that it was the presbytery that held the authority to determine who should be ordained. No denominational system could be allowed to compromise in any way that fundamental reality. Hence, this rather homogenized system of denominational and presbytery control evolved. Because ultimate presbytery authority it is asserted that a certain generality can serve best in the Form of Government. The candidate shall complete examination in "the areas covered by any standard ordination examination approved by the General Assembly."

One other contentious issue over the past quarter century appears at the end of the preparation section and the beginning of ordained service. In the years immediately after Reunion it was the cause of numerous overtures to amend. That is, where is ordination to be carried out? In the "northern stream", even as presbytery control was vigorously defended, the notion that ordination was for the whole church was stressed in the determination that ordination occurred in the "presbytery of care". In that view a person was prepared, examined, ordained and then "given" to the whole church to serve wherever the call had been issued. In the "southern stream" even as presbytery control was vigorously defended, the absolute right of a presbytery to determine its membership and to oversee the appropriateness of those called to serve its congregations led to the determination that ordination should be in the "presbytery of call".

The "presbytery of care" model is the more recent of the two, becoming prevalent only in the "northern stream" after 1958. Since 1983 the "presbytery of call" approach has become more common. The absolute right of a presbytery to determine its membership as won the debate. However, the option to negotiate between presbyteries that is permitted does complicate our practice. The extent to which these examinations are vigorous or perfunctory is not the question, we acknowledge that the presbytery has the right to determine its members, no Teaching Elder has an absolute right to serve by his or her choice alone.

Commissioning

As described above, in historical times the presbytery considered as a principle purpose the guarding of orthodoxy in the leadership of congregations. Thus, only fully qualified

Ministers of the Gospel (to use one of the old terms for the office) were placed in positions of responsibility within congregations. At the same time, the office of Ruling Elder was always seen as a spiritual office and it was expected that those who were ordained to this office were both able and willing to provide spiritual leadership to their own and other congregations as required. Such service was on an "as needed" basis and always under the supervision of the presbytery.

As for safeguarding the Word of God, the delegation of authority to Ruling Elders only went so far as to allow that an elder could be sent to preach at places where no fully ordained Minister was available. Such elders were titled "Commissioned Lay Preachers". A presbytery would choose from among qualified and willing elders one who would be commissioned to preach at a particular place for a particular period of time, presumably in some kind of accountable relationship to the presbytery through a committee charged with such oversight.

All that changed in the late 1990's when the scope of this commission was altered and the title changed to "Commissioned Lay Pastor"(CLP). The current language is virtually identical to the previous text with one exception. The content of areas of training for potential Commissioned Ruling Elders (the new title) is not specified, rather it need only be deemed appropriate to the position to be filled. This flexibility is appropriate and offers to presbyteries the opportunity to develop their own methods and guidelines.

On a broader level it does highlight the radical nature of the change in our historic polity that is the expansion of commissioned service to be accomplished. Where the tradition was that a qualified elder would be sought out to fill a specific need, now we are routinely training persons for unspecified needs, even for a "validated ministry of the presbytery" In other words, a CRE may be prepared for and authorized to do everything a Teaching Elder may do. Where that becomes quirky is that the notion of a validated ministry is a category of understanding created to deal with Teaching Elders called to service outside a pastoral ministry in a congregation; an interesting evolution indeed.

There is one aspect of the category of Commissioned Ruling Elder that is not addressed. It is an unresolved conundrum prevalent in many areas of the country. In the past decade or more there has come to be increasing pressure to find a way to establish "congregations" composed of gatherings of recent immigrants. Folk come to the USA from any number of countries and cultures where our missionaries have taught the ways of faith in a Reformed tradition. However, the particular gathering may have among them no persons who bear the office of elder from those communities. We want to recognize these folk in some way and support them in ministry. But without an "elder" there can be no designation of one being "commissioned". What to do?

The FOG does not give up the requirement that one must first be a Ruling Elder in order to be considered as a Commissioned Elder and serve such a ministry. I pray that presbyteries in their own mission strategies will be able to find sessions and congregations willing to take these immigrant fellowships under a wing and creatively identify those with the spiritual gifts and maturity to serve.

Certification

 The final section of Chapter Two deals with Certified Church Service. The topic as a matter of inclusion in the Form of Government is relatively recent and odd. It's persistence is, frankly, as much politically necessary as essential. The text begins with the idea that there are various ways in which individuals may pursue specialized training and attain recognition for their particular form of service to the church. Persons who obtain such certification through a process approved by the General Assembly shall receive certain blessings and benefits within the presbytery where they serve. The particular situation of Christian Educators is noted as current practice has several years of practice behind it.

Intense debate has surrounded the role of trained Christian Educators for years. In the Presbyterian Church in the United States in the year before Reunion, a Constitutional amendment was made to allow the ordination of Educators as a "fourth order of ministry". For the few hours between the convening of that final PCUS Assembly (when the change was acknowledged) and the convening of the First Assembly of the reunited PC(USA) when it disappeared those who had labored long and hard enjoyed the elevated status they desired.

The argument for a special status for educators takes its root in the writing of John Calvin, who envisioned such a fourth office, alongside ministers, elders and deacons. That no such office existed in Calvin's time, or has ever been maintained over time in our tradition does not take away from the importance of education or the work of educators. What is at stake in looking at the Form of Government is the role of such persons in governance. As the FOG defines "ordered ministries", along with rights and responsibilities comes accountability. Those who bear office place themselves under the authority of a council.

The text presents an interesting picture in this regard. First of all we look at the training and certification process. Educators speak with pride of the required education leading to certification. Indeed it is comprehensive and undeniably equivalent to or almost equivalent to that required of Teaching Elders. However, that training is developed, overseen and approved by a process that exists within the programmatic entities of the General Assembly. The process leading to certification and the accountability that may lead from it are not under the oversight of the bodies in which the certified person labors.

That leads then to the second curiosity. Representative councils composed of those in ordered ministries carry out Governance. Presbyteries govern through Teaching Elders who are members and commissioners who are Ruling Elders designated by the sessions of the congregations within the bounds and by Ruling Elders whom the presbytery by its own rule treats as members of the body by virtue of office or service to the presbytery. To serve in such *ex officio* capacities persons must be eligible for membership in the body, that is they must be Ruling Elders of congregations within the presbytery who could be commissioned to presbytery if the session so chose.

However, Certified Christian Educators are persons who have received training under the General Assembly, passed requisite examinations developed and administered by a General Assembly related entity and been certified by that same entity. There is no requirement that such persons be Ruling Elders in order to pursue and receive certification. As for receiving the right to speak at a meeting of the presbytery this presents no problem as the presbytery can grant anyone it wishes that right. Those who are Ruling Elders are eligible to be granted vote, in other words, the equivalent of full membership in the body, even though there no requirement that they be under the jurisdiction of a session within the presbytery.

Now the response will be that such concerns are far-fetched and to suggest that somehow the polity of the church is threatened by such persons is fear-mongering. That is not my intent although those who raise such concerns are often criticized as being opposed to Educators. The point is that foundational principles of governance are involved and those principles are compromised or diluted there needs be some understanding and acknowledgment of the risk.

Councils of the church

The opening sections of Chapter Three expand on the foundational understanding of the role, function, make-up and operation of councils of the church. Out of the mandate to revise with an eye toward the missional nature of the church and providing flexibility to its councils, the material in G-3.0106 warrants comment.

The whole of G-3.0100 describe that which is common to all councils. While the tasks required or expected of any particular council may vary, common to all is the task of "Administration of Mission". "Mission determines the forms and structures needed for the church to do its work." Each council must first determine its mission priorities before defining the forms and structures appropriate to carry it out. This is a significant change from the approach of the 1970s. At that time there was an attempt to control forms and structures from the highest level. The flow of resources were negotiated, but negotiated with the assumption that those resources were the General Assembly's to allocate. Structures were built into the Constitution with required committees prescribed in both form and purpose. The argument was that such parallel structures made administration consistent across the denomination. The current text seeks to assert with more clarity that each council has the authority and responsibility to define its mission and to structure itself to most effectively carry out that mission. Councils may continue the structures and titles to which we have become accustomed. But that will be the council's choice. The difference may seem subtle but it is significant.

All councils are expected to have manuals that define and describe how the mission is being accomplished. The drafting of such manuals is supported by those places in the FOG that define each council's responsibilities. To some this task is seen as burdensome. Wouldn't it be easier, they might say, if the Constitution itself, or at least the General Assembly through its staff and committees, just told us what to do? Yes, perhaps, were it not that such an approach would be in complete opposition to what the revision was asked to design and what the church has determined is needed. Each council must develop its own materials.

However, the work need not be burdensome. For most work, councils above the session likely already have policies and procedures in place that, in fact, are their handbooks. These may only need be collected, published and approved by the council. In other cases there may be documents prepared by others that can simply be adopted as "our own." The requirement for the session to have such a manual may be a bit more daunting. However, there is no requirement that the session have unnecessary policies and procedures. A session need only gather up any policies already in place and be conscientious about gathering in new policies as needs arise to conform to this requirement.

Funding the mission

"The funding of mission similarly demonstrates the unity and interdependence of the church." (G-3.0106) The text asserts above that the very existence of councils is a demonstration of the unity and interconnection of the church (3.0101). This sentence is the "put your money where your mouth is" assertion of the same point. I certainly know that pastors over the years have preached countless sermons asserting that contributions of "time, talent and **treasure**" (emphasis added) were marks of faithful connection to the Body of Christ. Why should it be any different for councils?

Indeed, the text of this section goes immediately on to say as much, *"failure of any part of the church to participate in the stewardship of the mission of the whole church diminishes that unity and interdependence."* This is the core principle. This is the primary and first assertion. This is the determination in light of which all subsequent assertions, discussions, requests and financial transfers are made. And, make no mistake about it, this was a point at which the drafting Task Force held long consideration and about which it received much feedback.

To state the obvious; the only money (the only resource of any sort, for that matter) available to the mission of the church, has its origin in the pew. (Assume that God has no grandchildren but that grandpa and grandma's money may have been invested by bequest to continue the work they supported when they physically occupied the fourth pew from the front on the right hand side.) The session is the council with the most onerous responsibility in determining the disposition of those dollars that are offered in gratitude to God.

Each council above the session is directed to prepare a budget. Presumably this "budget" is reflective of a mission plan. How these councils communicate to the session the needs for the mission of the "wider" church will determine the way the session approaches its task. As the session asks the people in the pew, so the sessions become the "pews" for the other councils. Ask and it shall be given, seek and you (may) find.

There remains one aspect of our financial stewardship that remains a "sticky wicket". What do we say about *per capita*? As described earlier the *per capita* system was common in parts of the church to fund, in earlier times, the essential ecclesiastical expenses of the councils. When this amount was relatively small it was not problematic. However, over time some components of the per capita budget and some shifts of expenses into it that could be construed as non-essential, or non-ecclesiastical, caused the amounts to rise and opposition to grow. Over the last generation judicial determinations have clarified (without satisfying anyone in particular) that session contributions of any sort are voluntary and that presbyteries are obligated to fulfill requests from synod and General Assembly. A presbytery may choose to make a separate and specific "ask" for funds based on the number of members a congregation reports, but that is the presbytery's option and there is no mechanism to force compliance upon the session.

That is the *status quo*. Some insist that maintaining a Constitutional reference to *per capita*, in those very words, is essential. It does not seem that those specific words are required, but they are still there. Councils are free to do what they have always done with or without specific fund raising mechanisms being constitutionally mandated.

Records and review

For those with an antiquarian bent, reading the session record books from years gone by and imagining how they were created can be a real treat. The clerk sat at the meeting with the minute book in his (likely not her) lap and with pen and ink wrote down the proceedings as they happened. Things are scratched out, inserted with little carets and marginal notations. A correction recorded at a later meeting might yield a strike through in the original posting. When something really needed to be removed the motion was to "expunge" it from the record, literally to pick it up off the page as if it had never been there.

Record keeping today is likely done on a computer with word processing software that allows vast latitude in editing and amending. To attempt to control the manner and means by which records are kept would be rather foolish given the rapid changes in technology. In olden days the rules specified that minutes were to be kept in a book with numbered pages. Presumably this kept people from major alteration of the record as the sequence of page numbers would be broken. As early as a generation ago however, I am aware of a clever secretary who purchased un-numbered pages for the "big book" and also a device to print numbers. No page was numbered until she had adjusted the computer file to her standard of perfection and caused it to be printed on the blank page that was then appropriately numbered!

So, what do we say about records? They are maintained because the body needs to know what it has done, and so that others can know that as well. The committee charged with relations with congregations may make a visit every few years to speak with the session. A Church Information Form may describe the congregation in the search for a new pastor. There may be any number of other ways in which the presbytery comes to know of the work and witness of a congregation. But it is the "records" of that Session that are submitted for review. The language describing General Administrative Review is broadly defined but all encompassing. Councils need to take seriously this process and ought to go well beyond merely verifying that meetings were opened and closed with prayer. In recent time this review has become far too perfunctory.

Sometimes I try to imagine what it would be like if the typical presbytery gathering to "review the minutes" had more than a check list. What if the reviewer, upon reading the notation at the May meeting that "MSC: Upon recommendation of the Education Committee, the new Junior High curriculum was approved." looked at the Clerk and said, "Tell me about that? Which curriculum was chosen and why did the session feel it was the best choice?" Would the Clerk remember? Had there actually been any discussion or rationale? I suspect that for many Clerks a suggestion would be made that someone else take the books to be reviewed next year. Or, perhaps, just perhaps, the Clerk would pay close attention and come to the review with a packet of documentation and committee reports to share just how conscientiously the session was taking care of its responsibilities! Yes, sometimes I try to imagine.....

Staff: an anomaly

A specific paragraph is inserted in the FOG (G-3.0110) that gives councils above the session the option to employ staff. Its insertion begs the question, "Who ever suggested that they could not?" Why the FOG answers a question that no one asked and simply grants privilege and authorization to councils to do what they would be perfectly free to do if it were not included is a bit mysterious. Does it constrain any behavior, or solve any problem? No.

What does it do? Well, it says that if you are going to hire staff you shall make provision in your manual for it. This manual provision shall include a process for electing executive staff (left undefined), position descriptions for all staff, methods of performance review and the manner of termination. In this day and age such matters would be routine for most persons chosen to oversee the work of a council, but perhaps it is good to spell them out as a mandated minimum expectation for the way we do business.

One phrase highlights a potential problem area. That phrase is "electing executive staff". In an earlier time there existed an agency of the General Assembly that provided support services for executive staff at all levels. It was in that time the provision for administrative staff first entered the Constitution. Never the less it is still here even though there is no longer a comparable national structure and more and more councils are abandoning "executive" labels for more general or pastoral descriptions of what staff is expected to do.

But the word at issue is "elected". There is a distinction to be made between persons who are "elected" by the body and those "hired" through a personnel process. We elect officers, such as a Moderator or a Clerk. We hire staff, such as a mission worker or a data entry clerk. The hired persons are governed by personnel policies. But, if an elected person is also paid, do the personnel processes for review and termination govern them? Or, are they subject only to the council? This problem comes into clear focus when the elected staff person is also a Teaching Elder who is "called" by the body. The current Committee on Ministry or any structure created for the purpose has a role to play in approving the call and in any proposed dissolution. Where do committees of a council come together in such cases? This was the historical reality that led to certain prescriptive and manual language to be inserted into the Constitution. This is the dilemma that must be anticipated as councils seek to develop their manuals of operation.

Sessions, presbyteries and synods

We now cast the language of councils into the framework of the Reformation Notes on the Nature of the Church. Each council works to fulfill the call to proclaim the Word, see to its sacramental life and rightly administer discipline (meaning not the rules of same but the nature of same). As a matter of style the formatting seeks to avoid a bullet point list in favor of a more narrative statement. The "shall" language is present and the assignments are as comprehensive as former lists, now framed in a way that challenges sessions and presbyteries to wrestle with the mission within their bounds and the mandates to be fulfilled.

Synods are a special matter. Whatever shall be done with synods? The move to large regional synods with programmatic oversight and some programmatic function that came to be in the 1970s has clearly not been a model that is helpful. Time and again the voices are raised suggesting that we just do away with synods. These calls continue. As a body derived from the presbyteries ending synods would change very little in the overall life of the denomination. But every cry to abolish synods is met with the equally loud response, how would we then replace what synods do that is essential?

Perhaps the most significant move for flexibility in the current text is the description for synods. Once approved by its presbyteries, a synod needs be minimally structured and responsible for as little as minute review and judicial functioning. What might a synod become? Discussions are ongoing to look seriously at the entire scope of middle governing bodies. More and more presbyteries are scaling back expectations for staff and programs as resources continue to dwindle. The notion that a presbytery would provide for every need is near extinction.

In days gone by presbyteries were smaller, perhaps less than 30 congregations in many instances. Synod boundaries were state boundaries for the sake of simplicity. Should presbyteries slip back into being communities of congregations who shared a more intimate lifestyle, synods could again come to the fore in providing supportive resources. The "shopping list" of needs includes: Mentoring of new pastors, training Ruling Elders for commissioning for special service, employing skilled persons as educators or administrators or stewardship trainers to strengthen leadership in congregations within the bounds of the synod. These are all functions that in an earlier age were synod-based services supported by national boards and agencies. With shared presbytery support, perhaps they could be so again. The language of the FOG easily allows for that to be.

The church and civil authority

The content of chapter 4 has been set apart to highlight that the church exists within the context of another law, the law of the civil society. Scripture directs that we are to exist within and under that law insofar as it does not compromise our freedom in the Gospel. By setting it apart in a separate chapter the FOG calls special attention to the ways in which councils of the church must take cognizance of the laws of the state or municipality within which they live.

The material on confidentiality and reporting are relatively new additions to our polity. Recent events calling attention to abuse in church settings make these essential. In some states church leaders are mandated to report to the state any suspicion of abuse. The specific provisions under which this mandate exists need to be carefully discussed with legal authorities in each setting. Pastors, particularly, may come into conflict with their own conscience when information is brought to them "in confidence". Because the confessional was a sacramental rite in some traditions, society has often extended a presumption of confidence to all pastors in hearing the "confessions" of parishioners. However, we do not hold to sacramental theology in that way. And, civil courts have been unpredictable in allowing pastors to remain silent. Again, while we are committed to maintaining relationships of confidence and trust, pastors are well advised to consult legal authorities for guidance.

The trust provisions in regard to property are introduced by a declaration that property is a tool for mission. This phrase is new and clarifies an assumption and sets the framework within which discussion of its use takes place. The reason this material was so strongly kept from revision is tied to the time in which it was first enacted. Careful study of laws among the states and court decisions in which the historic "assumed trust" relationship was called into question led to very carefully crafted language that would declare the position of the church and be understood in the civil courts. This was not a task for the faint of heart and casual alteration even for the most virtuous of purposes would be unwise.

The history is that church leaders had from the earliest days believed that property was a tool for mission of the congregation and the congregation was bound in a covenant with the church in such a way that should the members choose to leave, or violate the covenant in such a way as to be forced out, the property that had been gathered and provided by those who had gone before to further the work of the Presbyterian church would remain with the Presbyterian church or those that Presbyterian governance might designate. That principle was seen to be so implicit in the way we structured our polity that no one questioned it. And, civil courts accepted it, either because it was understood or because the court did not choose to meddle in church affairs. Then, that all changed.

When it changed, secular courts did choose to meddle. And, looking at our Constitutional documents they said, "Where does it say…?" And church leaders were forced to respond, "Well, it doesn't really say it, we've just always believed and practiced it." And the courts said, "Tough!" From that moment on, what had been assumed was written down and placed in the Constitution.

Ecumenicity and union

 The material in Chapter 5 greatly condenses previous wording. Our historic conviction and theological outlook clearly places us in a position open to other Christian bodies. We are not the whole church and we seek to fulfill Christ's high priestly prayer that we may be one. But how many of the specific procedures and practices need to be defined at a Constitutional level? As this activity is principally carried out at the level of the General Assembly or between individual congregations, normal review on a case by case basis seems most appropriate. Is that sufficient? The text assumes that it is. Basic definitions of relationships are provided with the assumption that manuals are sufficient to describe and prescribe the mechanics of how such relationships are created and to contain completed agreements.

Interpreting and amending

The Church (and our church) is an ever-changing body, growing and dying, reborn and adapting, responsive always to the movement of God's Spirit and the needs of God's people. Recognizing this as a reality we build into our Form of Government the ways in which we acknowledge that these assumptions about who we are and how we live together are not set in stone but will ever and always be interpreted and amended.

Interpretation results from specific actions of a General Assembly itself or as the result of a decision by the Permanent Judicial Commission of the General Assembly. If no current understanding of a point of confusion is available, councils of the church may direct a request for interpretation to the Stated Clerk of the General Assembly who will give it over to the Advisory Committee on the Constitution. That body will offer to the Assembly an interpretation, which can be received (hence accepted as adequate and appropriate) or altered or rejected by stating some other interpretation.

End Word

The vote of the presbyteries was hardly a landslide. Still, by May of 2011 the majority had voted in favor of adopting the proposed revision. On July 11, one year to the day after the close of the 219th General Assembly the Book of Order came to have four sections and the Foundations of Presbyterian Polity and Form of Government became our standards and guides. As a document these are only words on a page. As a statement of what the Holy Spirit is leading us to do and to be in this age it is a more complete pattern for living into the new reality we face than what we had before.

It has been a challenge and a joy to serve over the past 15 years at the center of this evolving discussion and document. God has blessed me with the opportunity to work with some of the finest and brightest and caring hearts and minds that could be assembled to such a task. I could have asked for, nor received, no finer Gift of Grace.

Made in the USA
Lexington, KY
12 October 2015